BENEFICIAL OWNERSHIP TRANSPARENCY IN ASIA AND THE PACIFIC

Ramandeep Chhina

DECEMBER 2022

ASIAN DEVELOPMENT BANK

ADB

Contents

Tables, Figures, and Boxes

Acknowledgments

This paper benefits greatly from the insights provided by experts, and from the discussions held during the joint Asian Development Bank (ADB) and Extractive Industries Transparency Initiative (EITI) Regional Workshop on Advancing Beneficial Ownership Transparency, conducted online from 21 to 23 February 2022.

The author, Dr. Ramandeep Chhina, would like to thank all the speakers at the regional workshop, and ADB and EITI colleagues, for their contributions to this research paper. The author is also grateful to the country experts for taking the time to participate in consultation meetings and sharing their valuable information on the current status of beneficial ownership transparency in their respective countries—notably Altynai Sydykova, Brenda Jay Angeles Mendoza, Carlo A. Garcia, Emanuel Bria, Erdenechimeg Dashdorj, Ferdian Ari Kurniawan, Frida Rustiani, Jose Luis Syquia, Lukas Alkan, Marie Gay Alessandra Ordenes, Mariya Lobacheva, Mark Burnett, Olesia Tolochko, and Shar Tsolomon.

Abbreviations

ACWG	Anti-Corruption Working Group
ADB	Asian Development Bank
AEOI	automatic exchange of information
AML/CFT	anti-money laundering/combating the financing of terrorism
BODS	Beneficial Ownership Data Standard
BOT	beneficial ownership transparency
CDD	customer due diligence
DNFBPs	designated nonfinancial businesses and professions
EITI	Extractive Industries Transparency Initiative
EOIR	exchange of information on request
EU	European Union
FATF	Financial Action Task Force
FIU	financial intelligence unit
GAIPSR	General Authority for Intellectual Property and State Registration, Mongolia
Global Forum	Global Forum on Transparency and Exchange of Information for Tax Purposes
LLC	limited liability company
MIID	Ministry of Industry and Infrastructure Development, Kazakhstan
MONEYVAL	Committee of Experts on the Evaluation of Anti-Money Laundering Measures and the Financing of Terrorism
MSG	multi-stakeholder group
OECD	Organisation for Economic Co-operation and Development
OGP	Open Government Partnership
PEP	politically exposed person
PNG	Papua New Guinea
SCIESU	State Committee on Industry, Energy and Subsoil Use, Kyrgyz Republic
SDG	Sustainable Development Goal
SEC	Securities and Exchange Commission, Philippines
UNCAC	United Nations Convention against Corruption
UNODC	United Nations Office for Drugs and Crime

Executive Summary

Beneficial ownership transparency (BOT) in regard to corporate entities is increasingly regarded as an essential element in the fight against corruption. It is a tool for preventing money laundering and countering the financing of terrorism and tax evasion. Numerous case studies have shown how corporate vehicles, such as corporations, trusts, foundations, and fictitious entities, can be used to improperly hide and transfer the proceeds of crime and conceal the identities of those who are involved in large-scale corruption. As a result, international efforts to prevent the misuse of corporate vehicles to commit financial crime have intensified.

Goal 16 of the Sustainable Development Goals, part of the 2030 Agenda for Sustainable Development adopted in 2015 by the United Nations General Assembly, recognizes that access to accurate and updated information on the beneficial owners of legal entities is a fundamental tool that can "substantially reduce corruption and bribery in all their forms." There are also international standards that require countries to take measures to ensure the transparency of the beneficial ownership of corporate entities in their jurisdictions. These standards include the Financial Action Task Force (FATF) Recommendations, the Extractive Industries Transparency Initiative (EITI), and the Global Forum on Transparency and Exchange of Information for Tax Purposes (the Global Forum).

This study analyzes the ongoing reforms, challenges, and opportunities in regard to ensuring BOT in nine developing member countries of the Asian Development Bank, which are also implementing countries of EITI. These are Armenia, Indonesia, Kazakhstan, the Kyrgyz Republic, Mongolia, Papua New Guinea, the Philippines, Tajikistan, and Timor-Leste. The study finds that the BOT regime and systems in the region are unevenly developed—ranging from countries that are at the very beginning of introducing the necessary legal and regulatory beneficial ownership reforms to countries that have made significant progress by establishing publicly accessible beneficial ownership registers.

The common issues that need to be addressed by these countries, depending on their level of progress, are also identified in the study. The objectives are to strengthen their national frameworks on ensuring BOT to align them with international standards, and to ensure the availability and accessibility of adequate, accurate, and up-to-date information on beneficial owners. Some of these issues include

(i)   a lack of an efficient and effective legal and regulatory framework that provides a strong legal basis for BOT;

(ii) technical and practical challenges to developing and implementing a beneficial ownership register, including data collection and data verification challenges;

(iii)   a lack of clarity on the interaction of the beneficial ownership disclosure regime with individuals' right to privacy and the data protection regime; and

(iv)   a lack of effective sanctions and enforcement mechanisms to ensure the accuracy of beneficial ownership information.

The study emphasizes the importance of delivering access to reliable and up-to-date information on beneficial owners; however, there are significant challenges to achieving this objective. In the interest of establishing and improving BOT, the study discusses (i) a range of topics for consideration that jurisdictions need to adequately address within their national frameworks and systems, (ii) the best practices on beneficial ownership reforms, and (iii) key practical considerations for policy makers and implementers within the region to further enhance their BOT reforms.

Countries in Asia and the Pacific are strongly encouraged to adopt a multipronged approach (i.e., using multiple sources of information on beneficial ownership such as a company approach, a registry approach, and an existing information approach) to enhance BOT and prevent the misuse of legal persons for criminal purposes. The use of a multipronged approach is widely recognized as an effective mechanism for ensuring the accuracy of beneficial ownership information by means of cross-checking. It also helps key stakeholders (including companies and reporting entities) identify any discrepancies or inconsistencies in the beneficial ownership information they have collected, by requesting information from different sources or by checking different registers.

This study identifies that establishing a register of beneficial owners of corporate vehicles is an emerging trend among jurisdictions worldwide. It is also widely recognized as a best practice for enhancing BOT and for ensuring beneficial ownership information is available and accessible to the competent authorities in a timely manner. Nonetheless, as highlighted by this study, such an approach needs to be complemented by other approaches and mechanisms to ensure the adequacy, accuracy, and reliability of the available beneficial ownership data and information.

I.   Introduction

Companies, trusts, foundations, partnerships, and a range of other corporate vehicles engage in a broad range of commercial operations. While these entities mostly play a vital and legitimate role in the economy, they are also often misused for illegal purposes. Criminals are drawn to corporate structures because of their intrinsic features, especially the separation of legal and beneficial ownership, which allows them to disguise the true ownership of, and conceal the illegitimate source of, funds and assets.

Various case studies and reports have demonstrated that corporate vehicles are misused to conceal the identities of known or suspected criminals, hide the true source or use of funds, and transfer the proceeds of crime between jurisdictions. Those studies and reports are published by organizations setting the international standards, including the Financial Action Task Force (FATF), the Organisation for Economic Co-operation and Development (OECD), the United Nations Office for Drugs and Crime (UNODC), and other leading institutions, as well as civil society organizations.

A 2001 OECD analysis found that nearly every economic crime involves the misuse of a corporate entity whose beneficial ownership is concealed.[1] According to a 2011 World Bank report that examined 200 grand corruption cases from around the world between 1980 and 2010, in more than 70% of these cases, anonymous companies were involved in facilitating corruption and hiding the gains, costing $56 billion over 3 decades.[2] A more recent report from the FATF and the Egmont Group, published in 2018, discovered that corporate entities, particularly anonymous shell companies, were a crucial element in 106 cases they had reviewed, allowing criminals to conceal their identities and illicit funds.[3]

Considering the risks associated with corporate vehicles in regard to concealing beneficial ownership, and to prevent their misuse for corruption, money laundering, terrorist financing, tax evasion, and other financial crimes, various initiatives have been taken at international and regional levels to ensure beneficial ownership transparency. These initiatives require that countries put in place effective mechanisms and systems to ensure the availability and accessibility of adequate, accurate, and up-to-date information on the beneficial owners of corporate entities. These initiatives include, for instance, the FATF Recommendations 2012, in particular, Recommendations 24 and 25, which establish international standards and provide important guidance to countries on BOT.

---

[1]   OECD. 2001. *Behind the Corporate Veil: Using Corporate Entities for Illicit Purposes*. Paris. p. 3.
[2]   Willebois, E. et. al. 2011. *The Puppet Masters: How the Corrupt Use Legal Structures To Hide Stolen Assets and What To Do About It*. World Bank and UNODC. https://star.worldbank.org/sites/star/files/puppetmastersv1.pdf.
[3]   FATF and Egmont Group. 2018. *Concealment of Beneficial Ownership*. Paris. https://www.fatf-gafi.org/media/fatf/documents/reports/FATF-Egmont-Concealment-beneficial-ownership.pdf..

These recommendations are further complemented by the continuous efforts within the framework of the Global Forum and the United Nations Convention against Corruption (UNCAC).

In December 2021, the UNCAC adopted a new resolution on beneficial ownership, encouraging states' parties to take measures to promote BOT and to ensure reliable beneficial ownership information is available and accessible to the competent authorities within their jurisdictions. The Extractive Industries Transparency Initiative (EITI) also introduced to its member countries a clear framework for enhancing BOT in the extractives sector (i.e., Requirement 2.5). At the regional level, significant and advanced BOT requirements have been imposed by the European Union (EU) Anti-Money Laundering Directives on the EU member states.

In line with international standards, particularly with the FATF Recommendations 2012, many jurisdictions have taken steps to introduce and implement various reforms in their beneficial ownership regime. The establishment of central beneficial ownership registers,[4] has emerged as one of the international best practices for enhancing BOT and ensuring beneficial ownership information is available and accessible to the competent authorities in a timely manner—although the approaches vary across jurisdictions.

For instance, a few countries, such as Indonesia, the United Kingdom, and Ukraine, have introduced beneficial ownership disclosure requirements simultaneously for all companies operating across the entire economy; while others, such as Armenia, and Slovakia, have initially prioritized beneficial ownership disclosures for one sector (e.g., the extractives sector or companies participating in public procurement purposes), with the potential to expand this to all industry sectors. Such reforms in beneficial ownership regimes enable countries to avoid reputational risks or negative ratings in the evaluations conducted by international institutions such as FATF, Global Forum, and EITI.

Nonetheless, due to the complexity of the concept of beneficial ownership, many countries have often raised concerns about the challenges they face in ensuring BOT, both at policy and technical levels. These are also reflected in the mutual evaluations conducted by the FATF, wherein, out of the 125 countries assessed worldwide against the FATF Recommendations between 2014 and early 2022, 70% were initially found *partially compliant* or *non-compliant* with Recommendation 24, and 65% were initially found *partially compliant* or *non-compliant* with Recommendation 25.[5]

---

[4]   Some countries that have introduced centralized beneficial ownership registers include, for instance, the United Kingdom, Ukraine, Belgium, Ireland, Indonesia, Denmark, and Australia.

[5]   These assessment ratings were given from 2014 until 22 March 2022. For further information, visit https://www.fatf-gafi.org/media/fatf/documents/4th-Round-Ratings.pdf (accessed 25 April 2022).

These statistics arise significantly for countries in the Asia and Pacific region, wherein, out of the 31 countries assessed against the FATF Recommendations during this period, the majority (83%) were initially found *partially compliant* or *non-compliant* with Recommendation 24, and 84% were initially found *partially compliant* or *non-compliant* with Recommendation 25.[6]

Considering the above background, this study analyzes the current legal and regulatory framework on BOT in a few countries in Asia and the Pacific, and highlights the common challenges in the region. The study identifies the ongoing reforms in countries in the region relating to BOT, the challenges they face, and the opportunities (or the next steps) that they should consider to enhance BOT in their respective jurisdictions. The study also highlights the best practices on beneficial ownership reforms, and offers practical guidance and recommendations or key considerations for governments in the region seeking to further enhance their BOT reforms. The countries covered within the scope of this study are Armenia, Indonesia, Kazakhstan, the Kyrgyz Republic, Mongolia, Papua New Guinea (PNG), the Philippines, Tajikistan, and Timor-Leste. These countries are developing member countries of the Asian Development Bank (ADB), as well as EITI implementing countries.

---

[6] These assessment ratings were from 2014 until 22 March 2022. The assessment ratings have changed in the follow-up reports of some jurisdictions in the Asia and Pacific region, resulting into 63% *partially compliant* or *non-compliant* countries with Recommendation 24 and 63% *partially compliant* or *non-compliant* countries with Recommendation 25. For further information, visit https://www.fatf-gafi.org/media/fatf/documents/4th-Round-Ratings.pdf (accessed 25 April 2022).

II. Methodology and Structure

This study is mainly based on a desk review of the relevant literature, both national and international, on ensuring the BOT of corporate entities in the selected countries. This includes (but is not limited to) (i) the laws and bylaws related to BOT for corporate entities in the selected countries; (ii) mutual evaluation reports by the Asia/Pacific Group On Money Laundering (APG), the Eurasian Group on Combating Money Laundering and Financing of Terrorism (EAG), and the Committee of Experts on the Evaluation of Anti-Money Laundering Measures and the Financing of Terrorism (MONEYVAL); (iii) the latest EITI validation reports; (iv) EITI Standard 2019 (especially Requirement 2.5); (v) the 2012 FATF Recommendations, the 2013 FATF Methodology, the 2014 FATF Guidance on Transparency of Beneficial Ownership, and the 2019 FATF Best Practices on Beneficial Ownership of Legal Persons; (vi) the 2019 OECD Guidelines on Transparency of Beneficial Ownership; and (vii) other relevant national and international literature as well as regional civil society and media reports.

The study has been further consolidated through consultation meetings with identified stakeholders from the selected jurisdictions (including Indonesia, Kazakhstan, the Kyrgyz Republic, Mongolia, and PNG) who are, or have been, involved in advancing BOT in their respective jurisdictions (Appendix 1). The information obtained from these meetings and the subsequent remote and desk research has informed the contents of this study. The study also greatly benefited from the discussions with, and insights provided by, experts during the joint ADB–EITI Regional Workshop on Advancing Beneficial Ownership Transparency, held from 21 to 23 February 2022 (Appendix 2).

The study is divided into six sections: Section 1 provides background information and an introduction to the study; Section 2 briefly discusses the methodology and structure; Section 3 highlights the relevant international standards on BOT as well as the status and compliance ratings of the selected Asia and Pacific countries against these standards; Section 4 discusses the ongoing reforms, challenges, and opportunities in regard to ensuring and enhancing BOT in the selected jurisdictions; Section 5 analyzes in detail the policy, technical, and practical considerations for beneficial ownership reforms, highlighting the best practices and offering recommendations; and Section 6 summarizes the findings and emphasizes the need for countries to adopt a multipronged approach to ensure beneficial ownership transparency.

III. Relevant International Standards on Beneficial Ownership Transparency

There are numerous international bodies and organizations focusing on BOT-related issues, each with a specific goal. Given the crucial role beneficial ownership information plays in combating corruption, money laundering, terrorist financing, and tax evasion, the G20's call for more integrated cooperation between organizations on this subject has been a significant development in recent years.[7] Accordingly, the FATF and the Global Forum, in particular, have started aligning their technical work on beneficial ownership more closely in recent years.

Table 1 provides an overview of the international framework covering beneficial ownership in the selected Asia and Pacific countries. The study later discusses some of these international standards in more detail, assessing the status and compliance rating of these countries against the BOT requirements within these standards.

Table 1: International Frameworks Covering Beneficial Ownership in Selected Asia and Pacific Countries (as of March 2022)

	FATF or FATF-Style Regional Bodies (MONEYVAL, APG, or EAG)	Extractive Industries Transparency Initiative (EITI)	The Global Forum	United Nations Convention against Corruption (UNCAC)	Open Government Partnership (OGP)	G20 Anti-Corruption Working Group (ACWG)
Armenia						
Indonesia						
Kazakhstan						
Kyrgyz Republic						
Mongolia						
PNG						
Philippines						
Tajikistan						
Timor-Leste						

APG = Asia/Pacific Group on Money Laundering, EAG = Eurasian Group on Combating Money Laundering and Financing of Terrorism , FATF = Financial Action Task Force, MONEYVAL = Committee of Experts on the Evaluation of Anti-Money Laundering Measures and the Financing of Terrorism, PNG = Papua New Guinea.

Source: Author.

---

7   OECD and IDB. 2019. *A Beneficial Ownership Implementation Toolkit*. p. 6. https://www.oecd.org/tax/transparency/beneficial-ownership-toolkit.pdf.

A. Financial Action Task Force

The Financial Action Task Force (FATF) is an intergovernmental body tasked with establishing international standards and encouraging the effective implementation of legal, regulatory, and operational measures to combat money laundering, terrorist financing, and other related threats to the integrity of the global financial system.[8]

Enhancing the transparency of legal persons and legal arrangements has long been a part of the FATF's priorities,[9] since these can be misused for illicit purposes by criminals who are trying to avoid anti-money laundering/combating the financing of terrorism (AML/CFT) measures by hiding the identity of beneficial owners. This is reflected not only in Recommendations 24 and 25 of the FATF Recommendations, as adopted in 2012, but also under various other recommendations, such as Recommendations 10 and 22, which require financial institutions and designated nonfinancial businesses and professions (DNFBPs) to identify and take reasonable measures to verify the identity of the beneficial owners of their customers. In March 2022, the FATF issued its revised Recommendation 24 to further strengthen the BOT measures.

The revised FATF Recommendation 24 and its Interpretive Note require countries to adopt a multipronged approach to ensure that the beneficial ownership information can be determined in a timely manner by the competent authorities. Countries have been given the discretion, based on a risk assessment, the context, and the materiality, to determine what form of beneficial ownership registry or alternative mechanism they want to adopt to ensure adequate, accurate, and current beneficial ownership information is available and accessible to the competent authorities. The FATF Recommendation 24 provides for the following approaches:

a. **The company approach** obliges corporate entities to obtain and maintain adequate, accurate, and up-to-date beneficial ownership information, and to make it available to the competent authorities in a timely manner.[10]

b. **The public authority or body approach** requires that the beneficial ownership information be held by a public authority or body (e.g., tax authority, financial intelligence unit, company registry, or beneficial ownership registry). Such information is not required to be held by a single body only. On the other hand, countries may choose the alternative mechanism approach, but there must be some specific mechanism that gives efficient access to beneficiary information. Relying on basic information or existing information alone is regarded insufficient.

---

[8]   Footnote 7, p. 7.

[9]   In 2003, the FATF became the first international body to set international standards on beneficial ownership. To address risks such as bearer shares and nominees and to provide more clarity on how countries should ensure information is accessible, these criteria were significantly reinforced in 2012.

[10]   In the case of express trusts or similar other legal arrangements, a similar obligation has also been placed on trustees or someone with an equivalent position in other legal arrangements under the FATF Recommendation 25. The Revised FATF Recommendation 24 also requires companies to cooperate with competent authorities to the fullest extent to determine the beneficial owner, as well as to cooperate with financial institutions and DNFBPs to provide adequate, accurate, and up-to-date information on the company's beneficial ownership information.

c. **The existing information approach** requires the regulators, stock exchanges, or reporting entities under under the AML/CFT law of the country law of the country (such as banks, lawyers, accountants, trusts, and company service providers) to collect and maintain the beneficial ownership information as part of their customer due diligence obligations, and to make it available to the competent authorities in a timely manner.[11]

As discussed above, countries are not obliged to establish a beneficial ownership register under the FATF Recommendations. This is just one of the mechanisms available to ensure that adequate, accurate, and up-to-date information on beneficial ownership is made available to the competent authorities in a timely manner in the country. Countries can either establish a register of beneficial ownership information (which can be held by a public authority or body, and this does not need to be a single body only), or they can use an alternative mechanism approach to ensure access to beneficial ownership information. The revised FATF Recommendation 24 and its Interpretive Note do not provide any further details on what this other alternative mechanism approach could be, but it is required that the alternative mechanism be specific and that reliance on basic or existing information alone is insufficient (footnote 11).

Compared with the previous FATF Recommendation 24, which requires countries to adopt one or more mechanisms (i.e., company approach, registry approach, or existing information approach) to achieve BOT, the revised FATF Recommendation 24 now requires countries to adopt a multipronged approach (i.e., a combination of approaches) to achieve the objective of ensuring BOT by making the beneficial ownership information available from different and complementary sources. This multipronged approach is fully supported by this study. According to a study conducted by the Transparency International, which analyzed the FATF mutual evaluation reports (MER) of 26 countries, in nearly 85% of the countries assessed, the competent authorities had only one source of beneficial ownership information available, which was mainly the one held by the reporting entities (i.e., financial institutions and DNFBPs under the AML/CFT law) when conducting their customer due diligence (CDD) checks.[12]

---

[11] FATF, 2012–2022. 2022. *International Standards on Combating Money Laundering and the Financing of Terrorism and Proliferation.* Paris (March). p. 93. https://www.fatf-gafi.org/media/fatf/documents/recommendations/pdfs/FATF%20Recommendations%202012.pdf. Hereinafter referred to as "The FATF Recommendations 2012."

[12] M. Martini. 2019. *Who is Behind the Wheel? Fixing the Global Standards on Company Ownership.* Transparency International. September. p. 13. https://images.transparencycdn.org/images/2019_Who_is_behind_the_wheel_EN.pdf; See also M. Martini. 2022. *Impact and Use of Beneficial Ownership Data.* Presentation made during ADB and EITI Regional Workshop on Advancing Beneficial Ownership Transparency. 21–23 February.

In all of these countries wherein the competent authorities had only one source of beneficial ownership information, the mutual evaluation reports revealed that the competent authorities faced significant challenges in accessing such information in a timely manner, and that there was a lack of access to accurate and reliable information (footnote 12).

Similar conclusions were also drawn by the FATF report on *Best Practices on Beneficial Ownership of Legal Persons* published in 2019.[13] The use of a multipronged approach increases transparency of, and access to, information through a variety of available sources and can help mitigate problems related to the accuracy of the available beneficial ownership information, by allowing for cross-checking.

More than 200 countries implement the FATF Recommendations, including the requirements under Recommendations 24 and 25, through an international network of FATF-affiliated regional bodies.[14] The FATF and its regional bodies conduct mutual evaluations, in accordance with the FATF's methodology, that assess a country's technical compliance with the FATF Recommendations and the effectiveness of its AML/CFT systems.[15] Table 2 provides the latest compliance ratings for the selected Asia and Pacific countries against Recommendations 24 and 25, as well as an assessment of the effectiveness of their AML/CFT systems in ensuring BOT against Immediate Outcome 5.

Table 2: Compliance with FATF Standards across Asia and the Pacific
(as of March 2022)

	Technical Compliance – Recommendation 24	Technical Compliance – Recommendation 25	Immediate Outcome 5
Armenia	Largely compliant	Largely compliant	Substantial effectiveness
Indonesia	Partially compliant	Partially compliant	Moderate effectiveness
Kazakhstan	N/A	N/A	N/A
Kyrgyz Republic	Largely compliant	Largely compliant	Moderate effectiveness
Mongolia	Largely compliant	Largely compliant	Low effectiveness
Papua New Guinea	N/A	N/A	N/A
Philippines	Largely compliant	Partially compliant	Low effectiveness
Tajikistan	Largely compliant	Partially compliant	Moderate effectiveness
Timor-Leste	N/A	N/A	N/A

FATF = Financial Action Task Force

continued on next page

---

13   FATF. 2019. Best Practices on Beneficial Ownership for Legal Persons. Paris. October. https://www.fatf-gafi. org/media/fatf/documents/Best-Practices-Beneficial-Ownership-Legal-Persons.pdf..

14   Footnote 7, p. 7.

15   FATF, 2013–2021. 2021. *Methodology for Assessing Technical Compliance with the FATF Recommendations and the Effectiveness of AML/CFT Systems.* Paris. October. pp. 65–70. https://www.fatf-gafi.org/media/fatf/documents/methodology/FATF%20Methodology%2022%20Feb%202013.pdf. Hereinafter referred to as "The 2013 FATF Methodology."

Table 2 (*continued*)

Notes:

1. N/A implies that the respective country has not yet been assessed against the 2012 FATF Recommendations.

2. The 2013 FATF Methodology provides for four levels of ratings, as used in Table 2, to assess a country's technical compliance with the FATF Recommendations: (a) *compliant*, which means there are no shortcomings; (b) *largely compliant*, which means there are only minor shortcomings; (c) *partially compliant*, which means there are moderate shortcomings; and (d) *non-compliant*, which means there are major shortcomings. To assess the level of effectiveness of the FATF Recommendations, the 2013 FATF Methodology provides for four ratings: (a) *high level of effectiveness*, which implies that the immediate outcome is achieved to a very large extent and minor improvements are needed; (b) *substantial level of effectiveness*, which implies that the immediate outcome is achieved to a large extent, but moderate improvements are needed; (c) *moderate level of effectiveness*, which implies that the immediate outcome is achieved to some extent and major improvements are needed; and (d) *low level of effectiveness*, which implies that the immediate outcome is not achieved, or achieved to a negligible extent, and fundamental improvements are needed.

3. Kazakhstan has not been evaluated against the 2012 FATF Recommendations. The last mutual evaluation of Kazakhstan was in 2011 against the previous 2003 FATF Recommendations and had its 4th Follow-Up Report published in 2016. The next round of mutual evaluation of Kazakhstan has been planned in Autumn 2022 against 2012 FATF Recommendations.

4. Papua New Guinea has not been evaluated against the 2012 FATF Recommendations. The last mutual evaluation of the country was against the previous 2003 FATF Recommendations and it was published in 2011.

5. Timor-Leste has not been evaluated against the 2012 FATF Recommendations. The last mutual evaluation of Timor-Leste was adopted in July 2012, and it was against the previous 2003 FATF Recommendations.

Source: Author.

B. Extractive Industries Transparency Initiative

The Extractive Industries Transparency Initiative (EITI) implements the global standard in regard to promoting transparent and accountable management of oil, gas, and mineral resources.[16] As of November 2021, 56 countries were implementing the EITI standard.

Requirement 2.5 of the EITI Standard 2019 requires EITI implementing countries to "maintain a publicly available register of the beneficial owners of corporate entities that apply for or hold a participating interest in an exploration or production oil, gas, or mining licence or contract, including the identities of their beneficial owners, the level of ownership, and details about how ownership or control is exerted."[17] In addition, any politically exposed persons (PEPs) who are beneficial owners are also required to adopt reporting obligations declaring ownership of mining, oil, and gas projects (footnote 17). The EITI Standard 2019 gave a deadline of 1 January 2020 for all EITI implementing countries to develop and publish comprehensive beneficial ownership disclosures for the extractives sector.

---

[16] See EITI. https://eiti.org (accessed 21 July 2022).

[17] Requirement 2.5, the EITI Standard, 2019. https://eiti.org/eiti-standard-2019 (accessed 30 June 2022).

The EITI has its own validation process, which is its quality assurance mechanism for assessing the ability of each EITI implementing country to meet the provisions of the EITI standard. The standard broadly includes country requirements relating to ensuring the transparency of contracts and licenses, production, revenue collection, revenue allocation, and social and economic spending.[18] The EITI validation model was last revised in December 2020. Among the countries covered by this study, only Armenia and the Philippines have undergone their validation under EITI's revised validation model to determine their progress in implementing the EITI Standard 2019. All other countries have been assessed so far only for their compliance with the 2016 Standard, under which Requirement 2.5 on BOT was only encouraged or recommended by EITI. As a result, this requirement was not taken into account in assessing compliance, and hence, no scorecard for their level of progress has been determined. Table 3 shows the recent validation results regarding the progress made by the selected Asia and Pacific countries on meeting Requirement 2.5 of the EITI standard.

Table 3: Progress Against Requirement 2.5 of the EITI Standard 2019 (as of March 2022)

	Latest Validation Report (Publication Date)	Progress against Requirement 2.5 of the 2019 EITI Standard
Armenia	June 2021	Satisfactory progress
Indonesia	July 2019	Not assessed yet
Kazakhstan	April 2020	Not assessed yet
Kyrgyz Republic	September 2020	Not assessed yet
Mongolia	February 2018	Not assessed yet
Papua New Guinea	October 2018	Not assessed yet
Philippines	June 2021	Mostly met
Tajikistan	November 2019	Not assessed yet
Timor-Leste	February 2018	Not assessed yet

EITI = Extractive Industries Transparency Initiative.
Source: Author.

---

[18]   The EITI Standard 2019. https://eiti.org/eiti-standard-2019.

C. Global Forum on Transparency and Exchange of Information for Tax Purposes

The Global Forum is tasked to ensure that its members and other relevant jurisdictions effectively follow and implement the international tax transparency standards. It has set standards for tax transparency that apply to both automatic exchange of information (AEOI) and exchange of information on request (EOIR). The Global Forum improved its EOIR tax transparency standard in 2015 by incorporating the requirement for beneficial ownership information availability in its revised Terms of Reference (2016), as stipulated by the FATF 2012 Standards.[19]

The EOIR standard integrates six FATF Recommendations that are directly related to the concept of beneficial ownership: (i) Recommendation 10 on CDD; (ii) Recommendation 11 on record-keeping; (iii) Recommendation 17 on reliance on third parties; (iv) Recommendation 22 on duty of care of DNFBPs; (v) Recommendation 24 on transparency and beneficial ownership of legal persons; and (vi) Recommendation 25 on transparency and beneficial ownership of legal arrangements.[20] On BOT, there are three key aspects that must be met by a jurisdiction under the EOIR standard: (i) Element A.1, ensuring the availability of beneficial ownership information for legal persons and legal arrangements; (ii) Element A.3, ensuring the availability of beneficial ownership information on bank account holders; and (iii) Element B.1, ensuring access to beneficial ownership information by the competent authority for EOI for tax purposes.[21] All of the Global Forum's member countries have agreed to implement the EOIR standard and participate in a peer review process to assess its effective implementation.

Both the AEOI standard and the EOIR standard include the concept of beneficial ownership, which is described similarly as with the FATF standards, and serve as a basis for financial accounts reporting.[22] As a result, the reporting financial institutions are required to identify the beneficial owners, including the country of tax residence, of certain financial accounts, and, if necessary, report this information to partner tax authorities (footnote 7). While more member countries are preparing to participate in AEOI in the near future, more than 100 countries have already committed to exchanging this information on an annual basis.[23]

---

[19] Footnote 7, p. 6.
[20] The Global Forum. 2021. *Building Effective Beneficial Ownership Frameworks: A Joint Global Forum and IDB Toolkit.* Paris: OECD Publishing. pp. 9, 12. https://www.dian.gov.co/impuestos/RUB/Documents/Building-Effective-beneficial-ownership-frameworks.pdf.
[21] Footnote 20, p. 23. For the purposes of this study, Element A.1 of the EOIR is the most relevant that relates to ensuring the availability of beneficial ownership information of legal persons and legal arrangements.
[22] Footnote 7, p. 6.
[23] Footnote 7, p. 7; See also The Global Forum. 2022. *Automatic Exchange of Information (AEOI): Status of Commitments* (as of January 2022). https://www.oecd.org/tax/automatic-exchange/commitment-and-monitoring-process/AEOI-commitments.pdf.

The EOIR standard provides for the following approaches to ensure the availability of beneficial ownership information:

(i)   existing information or AML/CFT approach, requiring financial institutions and DNFBPs under the AML/CFT law of a country (such as banks, lawyers, accountants, trusts, and company service providers) to collect and maintain the beneficial ownership information as a part of their CDD obligations.

(ii)   company approach, obliging corporate entities to obtain and maintain adequate, accurate, and up-to-date beneficial ownership information.

(iii) central beneficial register approach, requiring that a beneficial ownership register be held by a public authority.

(iv)   tax authority approach, requiring that the beneficial ownership information be kept by the tax authority of the country.

As shown in Figure 1, of the 15 Asia and Pacific countries reviewed by the Global Forum under the EOIR standard,[24] 10 countries or 66.7% used two or more approaches for the availability of beneficial ownership information, and only 5 countries or 33.5% used only one approach (i.e., AML/CFT approach).[25]

Figure 1: Beneficial Ownership Approaches Used by 15 Asia and Pacific Countries Reviewed by the Global Forum

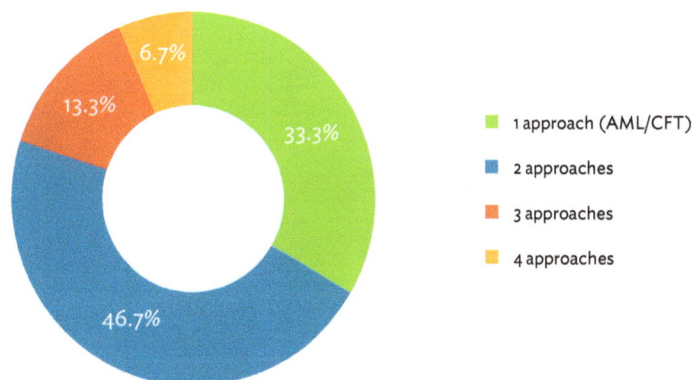

AML/CFT = anti-money laundering and combating financing of terrorism.
Source: Hamadi, H. 2022. *Policy Approaches for Beneficial Ownership Implementation*. Presentation made during ADB and EITI Regional Workshop on Advancing Beneficial Ownership Transparency. 21–23 February.

Figure 2 and Figure 3 summarize the determinations and ratings received by the 15 Asia and Pacific countries per number of approaches used.

---

[24]   These include Brunei Darussalam, the Federated States of Micronesia, India, Indonesia, Japan, Kazakhstan, Malaysia, the Marshall Islands, the People's Republic of China, Nauru, the Philippines, PNG, Samoa, Singapore, and Vanuatu.

[25]   Hamadi, H. 2022. *Policy Approaches for Beneficial Ownership Implementation*. Presentation made during ADB and EITI Regional Workshop on Advancing Beneficial Ownership Transparency. 21–23 February.

Figure 2: Determination of the Legal Framework

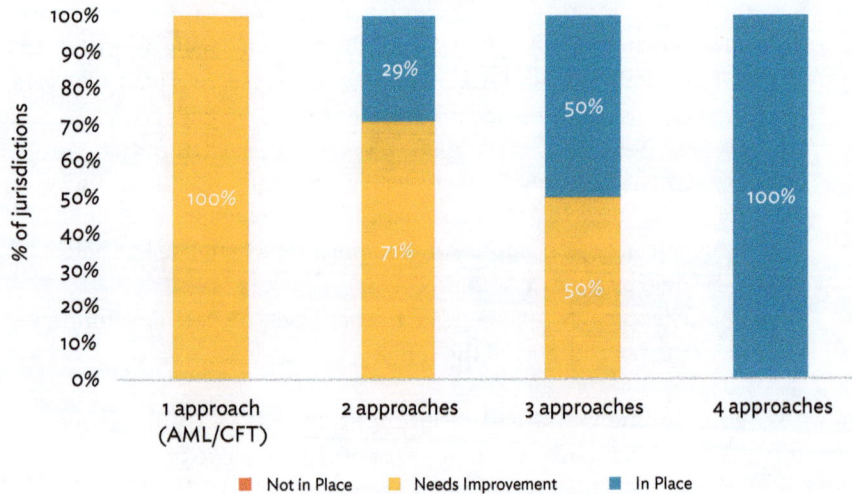

AML/CFT = anti-money laundering/combating financing of terrorism.
Source: Hamadi, H. 2022. *Policy Approaches for Beneficial Ownership Implementation*. Presentation made during ADB and EITI Regional Workshop on Advancing Beneficial Ownership Transparency. 21–23 February.

Figure 3: Rating of Practical Implementation

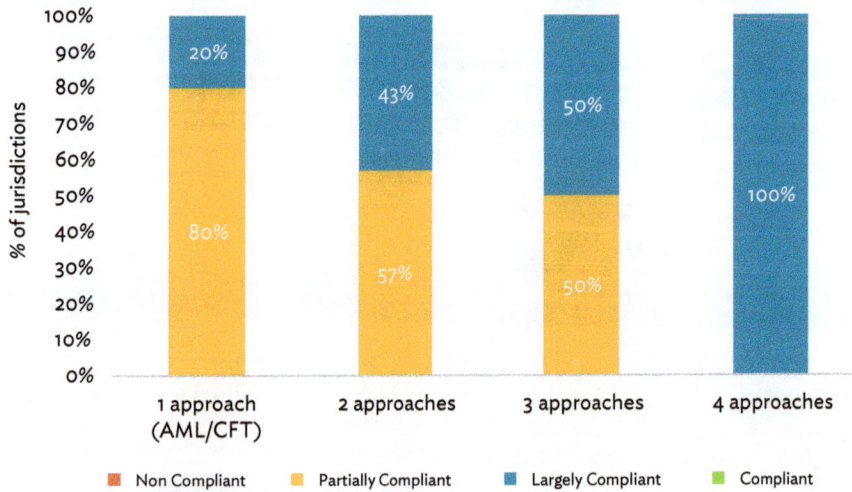

AML/CFT = anti-money laundering/combating financing of terrorism
Source: Hamadi, H. 2022. *Policy Approaches for Beneficial Ownership Implementation*. Presentation made during ADB and EITI Regional Workshop on Advancing Beneficial Ownership Transparency. 21–23 February.

Table 4 provides the results of recent peer reviews of the selected Asia and Pacific countries for this study against the requirements of the EOIR standard on the availability of legal and beneficial ownership information.

Table 4: Compliance with the Beneficial Ownership Requirement of the EOIR Standard (as of March 2022)

	Latest Peer Review Report (year)	A1 – Ownership and Identity Information
Armenia	Not yet reviewed	NA
Indonesia	2018	Partially compliant
Kazakhstan	2018	Partially compliant
Kyrgyz Republic	Not a member of the Global Forum	NA
Mongolia	Not yet reviewed	NA
Papua New Guinea	2020	Partially compliant
Philippines	2018	Partially compliant
Tajikistan	Not a member of the Global Forum	NA
Timor-Leste	Not a member of the Global Forum	NA

EOIR = exchange of information on request, NA = not applicable.

Notes: The Global Forum ratings, as provided in Table 4, have the following interpretations: (a) *compliant* means the EOIR standard is implemented. This rating can be granted even if a few recommendations were issued, to the extent that no material deficiencies were identified; (b) *largely compliant* means the EOIR standard is implemented to a large extent, but improvements are needed. Some deficiencies identified are material but have limited impact on EOIR; (c) *partially compliant* means the EOIR standard is only partly implemented. At least one material deficiency which has had, or is likely to have, a significant effect on EOIR in practice has been identified; and (d) *non-compliant* implies that fundamental deficiencies in the implementation of the EOIR standard have been identified.

Source: Author.

During the joint ADB–EITI beneficial ownership workshop, Hakim Hamadi from the Global Forum highlighted some of the lessons learned from the EOIR peer reviews on ensuring BOT (footnote 25), as also noted in the 2021 Global Forum Technical Assistance Report on Chile on *Options to Implement a Beneficial Ownership System.*[26] The lessons learned include the following:

(i)   Using various legal frameworks and a multipronged approach (i.e., using various sources of information on beneficial ownership), particularly the AML/CFT framework combined with one or more approaches, generally leads to a more solid beneficial ownership system. However, the overall number of jurisdictions using a multipronged approach is still limited.

(ii) Using a multipronged approach does not automatically lead to efficient beneficial ownership systems unless the legal framework is aligned with international standards and is effectively enforced with strong monitoring and supervision.

[26]   The Global Forum. 2021. *Chile Technical Assistance Report: Options to Implement a Beneficial Ownership System.* April. https://www.pauta.cl/pauta/site/docs/20211008/20211008163925/chile_technical_assistance_report_options_to_implement_a_beneficial_ownership_system_final.pdf.

(iii)   Using central beneficial ownership registers is a growing trend and has the benefit of centralizing the information with one authority and has other advantages, including

- combined synergies with the AML/CFT and company approaches;
- ensuring real-time access to beneficial ownership information, subject to conditions and criteria, for other persons (e.g., AML/CFT-obliged persons, any person with a legitimate interest or even the general public); and
- improving the quality of beneficial ownership information and the supervision of obligations, wherein persons with access to the register must report discrepancies, law enforcement authorities must supervise compliance of AML/CFT-obliged persons and entities with their beneficial ownership obligations, and the authority responsible for the register must carry out at least formal control of the declaration and identification of non-compliant entities.[27]

The establishment of a central beneficial ownership register has been widely recognized as a growing trend and a best practice for ensuring BOT.[28] Importantly, however, the establishment of a beneficial ownership registry alone will not guarantee its effectiveness. As mentioned above, and as stated in the FATF best practices paper,[29] to ensure the accuracy and reliability of the beneficial ownership information within the register, a combination of different approaches and features is needed (see Section 5).

D. United Nations Convention against Corruption

The United Nations Convention against Corruption (UNCAC) came into force on 14 December 2005 and had 140 signatories and 188 state parties as of 31 March 2022. The UNCAC encourages BOT among its state parties. Article 12 (1) of the UNCAC requires that "each State party shall take measures, in accordance with the fundamental principles of its domestic law, to prevent corruption involving the private sector."[30] Such measures may include, among other things:

> Promoting transparency among private entities, including, where appropriate, measures regarding the identity of legal and natural persons involved in the establishment and management of corporate entities (footnote 30).

The UNCAC also provides for the Implementation Review Mechanism to assist the state parties to effectively implement the provisions of the Convention. The first cycle

---

[27]   Footnote 26, pp. 78–79.
[28]   Harari, M. et al. 2020. Ownership Registration of Different Types of Legal Structures from an International Comparative Perspective: State of Play of Beneficial Ownership – Update 2020. *Tax Justice Network.* 1 June. p. 18; Per this report, 81 jurisdictions worldwide have started implementing a beneficial ownership registry approach, in addition to relying on the company and existing information approaches, by requiring legal entities to file beneficial ownership information with a government authority.
[29]   Footnote 13, p. 22.
[30]   UNCAC, Article 12(1). https://www.unodc.org/documents/brussels/UN_Convention_Against_Corruption.pdf.

of the UNCAC Implementation Review Mechanism started in 2010 and covered the chapters of the Convention on criminalization, law enforcement, and international cooperation. In 2015, the second cycle of the UNCAC Implementation Review Mechanism started assessing the state parties' implementation of Chapters II and V of the UNCAC, including Article 12 of the UNCAC, which promotes BOT.[31]

In December 2021, at the Ninth Congress of State Parties to the UNCAC, the state parties approved the new Resolution 9/7 on enhancing BOT, titled "Enhancing the use of beneficial ownership information to facilitate the identification, recovery and return of proceeds of crime." This new UNCAC resolution on beneficial ownership is an important step toward broadening support for beneficial ownership reforms, in line with the FATF Recommendations 2012, and toward promoting BOT among the UNCAC state parties.[32] Some of the elements of the UNCAC Resolution 9/7 on BOT include the following:

(i)   Calling upon state parties to ensure, or to continue ensuring, efficient access to adequate and accurate beneficial ownership information on companies in a timely manner for their domestic central or competent authorities, including financial intelligence units (FIUs) and tax administrations, in accordance with domestic law.

(ii)   Encouraging state parties to collect and maintain beneficial ownership information for legal persons and legal arrangements, where appropriate and in accordance with the fundamental principles of their domestic legal systems and domestic law.

(iii) Calling on state parties to adopt a multipronged approach to BOT through appropriate mechanisms such as registries that provide efficient access to adequate and accurate beneficial ownership information on legal persons and legal arrangements in a timely manner.

(iv)   Encouraging state parties to consider developing effective mechanisms whereby relevant domestic authorities and entities can verify or check the beneficial ownership information provided by legal persons and legal arrangements, and to ensure that they have the necessary mandate or authorities for that purpose (footnote 32).

E. Open Government Partnership

The Open Government Partnership (OGP) is a voluntary global initiative or partnership which came into existence in 2011, bringing together governments and civil society to promote transparent, participatory, inclusive, and accountable governance. At the end of July 2022, the OGP included 77 countries, 106 local governments, and thousands of civil society organizations as members.[33]

---

[31]   For further details on the findings of each completed UNCAC Implementation Review for various countries, visit UNODC. Implementation Review Mechanism. Country Profile Pages. https://www.unodc.org/unodc/en/corruption/implementation-review-mechanism.html (accessed 25 April 2022).

[32]   See UNCAC Resolution 9/7 on Beneficial Ownership. https://www.unodc.org/unodc/en/corruption/COSP/session9-resolutions.html#Res.9-7.

[33]   See Open Government Partnership. https://www.opengovpartnership.org/our-members/.

Upon joining the OGP, countries or governments make a commitment to develop an action plan that outlines how they will co-create and put into practice specific open government reforms to strengthen governance, fight corruption, empower citizens, and promote transparency.[34] The Independent Reporting Mechanism, established by the OGP, oversees all action plans to ensure governments adhere to their commitments. BOT has been reported as a rapidly growing thematic area in OGP action plans. In 2013, only one country, the United Kingdom, included BOT in its OGP action plan, whereas now, more than 25 countries do.[35] These BOT commitments in action plans range from creating extractives sector company registers to establishing public and open central registers to ensure that data in beneficial ownership registers is validated.

The OGP also established the Beneficial Ownership Leadership Group in 2019 to support the implementation of BOT through the OGP and other platforms. This group currently consists of Armenia, Kenya, Latvia, Mexico, the Slovak Republic, and the United Kingdom.[36] Each country commits to a set of best practice disclosure principles when they join the Beneficial Ownership Leadership Group. The OGP has also established various subregional and regional communities of practice for peer learning on BOT, including in Latin America, the Western Balkans, and the Eastern Partnership, to help countries learn from each other's experience on initiating and implementing BOT reforms. Within the Asia and Pacific region, 12 countries are members of the OGP, including Armenia, Australia, Azerbaijan, Georgia, Indonesia, the Kyrgyz Republic, Mongolia, New Zealand, the Philippines, PNG, the Republic of Korea, and Sri Lanka.

F. G20 Anti-Corruption Working Group

Established in 2010, the G20 Anti-Corruption Working Group (ACWG) reports on corruption prevention to the G20 leaders. Among the thematic focus areas of the ACWG are public and private sector integrity and transparency, and BOT. In 2014, the G20 issued the High-Level Principles on BOT. The G20 members are committed to promoting greater BOT by adhering to these principles and the accompanying national implementation plans, as well as to the international FATF standards on transparency of beneficial ownership of legal persons and arrangements.[37]

---

[34] Open Government Partnership. Open Government Declaration. https://www.opengovpartnership.org/process/joining-ogp/open-government-declaration/.

[35] Open Government Partnership. OGP's Approach to Peer Exchange: The Example of Beneficial Ownership. https://www.opengovpartnership.org/stories/ogps-approach-to-peer-exchange-the-example-of-beneficial-ownership/.

[36] See Open Government Partnership. Beneficial Ownership. https://www.opengovpartnership.org/policy-area/beneficial-ownership/.

[37] G20 ACWG. 2021. *Anti-Corruption Accountability Report 2021*. Rome. p. 4. https://www.unodc.org/documents/corruption/G20-Anti-Corruption-Resources/Accountability-and-Monitoring-Reports/2021_G20_ACWG_Accountability_Report_2021.pdf.

Each year, the G20 Accountability Report assesses the progress made by G20 countries against the commitments made by the Group in various thematic areas, including BOT. The G20 ACWG Accountability Report 2020 highlighted that "the maintenance of BO [beneficial ownership] information remains an area with comparatively low compliance, even among jurisdictions that have signed up to global standards such as the FATF Recommendations 2012 and the G20 High-Level Principles on BOT."[38]

The G20 ACWG Accountability Report 2021 assessed the progress made by G20 countries against three main areas: (i) BOT, (ii) private sector transparency and integrity, and (iii) integrity and liability of legal persons.[39] In the area of BOT, the report identified that although a growing number of countries have introduced BOT legislation, the lack of effective verification processes for beneficial ownership information remains a major obstacle to the effective use of this information.[40] The report also highlighted that one of the most common ways chosen by G20 member countries to enhance BOT is "the use, or the commitment to introduce, automated cross-checking of data from various government databases to verify BO [beneficial ownership] data prior to allowing a legal entity to be registered, exploiting the possibilities offered by IT, and/or setting up a dedicated agency or service to bring together in one place the different registers managed by the various national entities" (footnote 37).

---

[38]   Footnote 37, p. 6.
[39]   Footnote 37, p. 4.
[40]   Footnote 37, p. 7.

IV. Beneficial Ownership Transparency in Selected Asia and Pacific Countries

This section provides a brief overview of the status of BOT in the selected Asia and Pacific countries and discusses the ongoing reforms, challenges, and opportunities in regard to ensuring and enhancing BOT in each jurisdiction.

A. Armenia

To make its beneficial ownership data more accessible, Armenia has established a legal framework for beneficial ownership disclosures; and an online register is being created to improve the usability of the country's beneficial ownership data.[41] The Republic of Armenia Law On State Registration of Legal Entities Separated Divisions of Legal Entities, Institutions and Individual Entrepreneurs (hereinafter the "Law on State Registration of Legal Entities") requires all legal entities in Armenia to provide beneficial ownership information to the State Unified Register of Legal Persons (the State Register), which is maintained by the Ministry of Justice. With the exception of personally identifiable information, the State Register is in charge of making the beneficial ownership information publicly available.[42] Armenia committed to establishing an open and public beneficial ownership as a part of the OGP action plan for 2018–2020 (footnote 41). The relevant laws in Armenia went through a series of amendments between 2018 and 2020 to clearly define the term "beneficial owner" and establish a comprehensive sector regulatory framework for the disclosure of beneficial owners (footnote 41).

In line with international best practices, the definition of "beneficial owner(s)" as provided by the Law on State Registration of Legal Entities includes both the components of ownership and control interests, and provides a solid foundation for requiring beneficial ownership disclosure.[43] The Law on State Registration of Legal Entities defines the term "beneficial owners" as natural persons who (i) directly or indirectly own more than 20% of the voting shares or stocks of the legal entity, or directly or indirectly own more than 20% of the authorized capital of the legal entity;

---

[41] EITI. 2021. *Validation of Requirement 2.5 – Armenia: Final Assessment by the EITI International Secretariat.* Oslo. 23 March. p. 2.

[42] Footnote 41, p. 3.

[43] It should be noted that the Law on State Registration of Legal Entities does not give the definition of the "beneficial owner," but it contains a reference to the definition of "beneficial owner" as provided under Article 3 (1)(14) of the Law on Combating Money Laundering and Terrorism Financing of the Republic of Armenia.

(ii) exercise real (de facto) control over the legal entity by other means; or (iii) are officials who carry out the general or current management of the activity of the legal entity if there is no natural person meeting the abovementioned requirements under (i) and (ii).[44]

The first round of beneficial ownership disclosures was conducted in Armenia in the last quarter of 2019.[45] Initially, all companies applying for or holding mining permits in the extractives sector were required and requested to report their beneficial ownership information to the State Register.[46] In 2020, this information was submitted in paper format and disclosed in PDF file type, as the online register was still being developed.[47] The beneficial ownership declaration form requires information on the identity (identities) of the respective beneficial owner(s), including "nationality, full name, date of birth, serial number and date of issue of the ID document, registered address, place of residence, contact details, and identification of PEPs, as well as closely affiliated persons, the level of ownership, and details about how ownership or control is exerted."[48] The declaration form also has a data section where the name of the stock exchange and a link to the stock exchange filings for publicly traded companies can be included.[49] Except for personal information like ID document details, registration details, residential addresses, and contact information, the majority of the information is freely accessible to the public.[50]

Armenia has collaborated with Open Ownership to develop an online portal for beneficial ownership disclosures. With an initial focus on extractive industries, in 2021, Armenia began publishing beneficial ownership data in line with the Beneficial Ownership Data Standard (BODS) via its company register.[51] Structuring data in line with the BODS can help support automated data verification; for example, information about Armenia's citizens is automatically compared and checked against the database of passport holders.[52] Since March 2021, legal entities have been required to submit electronic beneficial ownership declarations to the online beneficial ownership register.[53]

---

[44] Gabuzyan, K. 2022. *BO Disclosure: Experience of the Republic of Armenia*. Presentation made during ADB and EITI Regional Workshop on Advancing Beneficial Ownership Transparency. 21–23 February 2022.

[45] The legislative amendments became effective on 1 July 2019, thereafter, metal mining companies were obliged to submit their first declarations on beneficial owners to the state register no later than 30 November 2019.

[46] Footnote 41, p.3.

[47] Footnote 41, p. 2.

[48] Footnote 41, pp. 3, 12.

[49] Footnote 41, pp. 3–4.

[50] Footnote 41, p. 4.

[51] Open Ownership. 2021. *Armenia and Latvia Become First Countries to Publish Data in Line with the Beneficial Ownership Data Standard*. September. https://www.openownership.org/blogs/armenia-and-latvia-become-first-countries-to-publish-data-in-line-with-the-beneficial-ownership-data-standard/.

[52] Footnote 41, p.3.

[53] EITI. 2021. *The 2021 EITI Armenia Annual Conference Took Place on 23 July*. https://www.eiti.am/en/news/2021/07/23/2021-eiti-armenia-annual-conference-took-place-on-23-july/111/.

The State Register verifies the accuracy of the declaration forms' completion, and if inconsistencies are found, it informs the Ministry of Territorial Administration and Infrastructure (MTAI).[54] The Ministry has the authority to impose sanctions or take remedial action against companies in the extractive industries if they failed to comply with the requirement to provide beneficial ownership information to the State Register, or if they submitted incomplete or false information. If any stakeholder, including individuals, has a reasonable suspicion that the information has been falsified, they can alert the authorized body (footnote 41).

In June 2021, Armenia adopted a set of laws that widened the scope of companies obliged to disclose their beneficial ownership information to the register. These laws also provided for reforming the process of beneficial ownership disclosure. In particular, legal entities operating in the regulated sector of public utilities and in the audiovisual media sector were obliged to disclose beneficial ownership data beginning 1 September 2021.[55] This obligation then came into effect for all other legal entities from 1 January 2022, except for limited liability companies (LLCs) with only natural persons as participants (footnote 55). Beginning 1 January 2023, LLCs with only natural persons as participants and non-commercial organizations will also be required to disclose their beneficial owners (footnote 55). Under the new regulations, exceptions have been established for legal entities registered by the Central Bank (footnote 55).

The expansion of the beneficial ownership disclosure regime to all sectors beyond the mining sector might prove to be challenging for the country in various ways, in terms of resource constraints (both technical and human), data collection, and verification. Capacity-building activities on a wider scale for companies might also be needed, to provide guidance on reporting beneficial ownership data to the registry, as well as capacity building to improve the use and analysis of beneficial ownership data by relevant stakeholders and authorities. Work is also ongoing to strengthen the verification procedures and data quality in the online register, including through process automation and additional consultations with companies.

B. Indonesia

Indonesia has established a central registry of beneficial owners. The Ministry of Law and Human Rights is responsible for hosting the registry. All corporations are required to submit reports to the registry and keep their beneficial owner information up-to-date on a regular basis.

---

54   Footnote 41, p. 16.
55   EITI. 2021. *Who is the Beneficial Owner? The National Assembly of RA Adopted the Package of Laws on Disclosure of the Beneficial Owners in Armenia.* https://www.eiti.am/en/news/2021/06/23/who-is-the-beneficial-owner-the-national-assembly-of-ra-adopted-the-package-of-laws-on-disclosure-o/108/.

A "corporation" is defined by Presidential Regulation No. 13/2018 as any organized group of people or assets, whether or not it has been constituted as a legal entity. This definition includes LLCs, foundations, associations, cooperatives, limited and unlimited partnerships, and any other types of corporations. The information on beneficial owners that is required to be reported to the central registry includes "their full name, passport/national ID registration number, place and date of birth, nationality, residential address, foreign residential address (if residing in a foreign country), tax identification number, and the relationship between the legal person and the beneficial owner(s)."[56] Beneficial ownership information is required to be updated annually, and any changes are required to be reported within 3 working days. The Ministry of Law and Human Rights noted that, as of 28 November 2021, 584,790 out of 2,386,506 corporations (24.5%) had disclosed beneficial ownership information to the central registry.[57]

However, there remains a lack of adequate verification mechanisms to ensure that the beneficial ownership information disclosed by corporations and contained in the central registry is accurate and up-to-date. One control mechanism is a public notary is required to incorporate a company in Indonesia; however, notaries are not required to update the beneficial ownership information held within the register. The effectiveness of this verification system is also called into question by the fact that notaries show very formal and limited understanding of the beneficial ownership concept and identification when they perform their customer due diligence (CDD) checks on their customers. Under Article 13 of Presidential Regulation No. 13/2018, the Ministry of Law and Human Rights has been given a legal mandate to verify the beneficial ownership data within the register. However, the law also mentions other ministries and state agencies that can verify the beneficial ownership data of companies in their specific sectors, including the Ministry of Small and Medium Enterprises, the Ministry of Trade, and other state agencies that have supervisory roles over companies, such as the FIU and the Anti-Corruption Commission.

According to Article 12 of Regulation No. 21/2019 on "Supervisory Procedures: Application of the Principle of Identifying the Beneficial Owners of the Corporation," sanctions are applicable for late submission or non-compliance with the beneficial ownership disclosure requirements. These sanctions range from removing access to the online registry portal to recommending that responsible ministries and public authorities delay, revoke, or cancel the corporation's business license.[58] There is also a criminal penalty of up to 7 years of imprisonment for knowingly providing false information.[59] In principle, the beneficial ownership information is accessible to the public, as provided by the law. However, access to the online registry is available

---

56   UNODC. 2020. *Beneficial Ownership Regulations and Company Registries in Southeast Asia: Analysis of Regulatory Deficiencies.* Vienna.

57   Berek, F. 2022. *BO Data Collection, Integration, Disclosure and Use.* Presentation made during ADB and EITI Regional Workshop on Advancing Beneficial Ownership Transparency. 21–23 February 2022.

58   Article 12, Regulation No. 21/2019 on Supervisory Procedures: Application of the Principle of Identifying the Beneficial Owners of the Corporation.

59   Section 241 of the Penal Code. See OECD. 2018. *Peer Review Report on the Exchange of Information on Request: Indonesia.* The Global Forum on Transparency and Exchange of Information for Tax Purposes, Second Round. p. 44.

only after registering with the portal and after paying a fee of about $3.00 for each information request. During consultation meetings, authorities stated that the only information from the online registry accessible to the public is the legal ownership information (i.e., not the beneficial ownership information).

The Ministry of Energy and Mineral Resources and the Ministry of Agriculture also require corporations within their ambit to disclose their beneficial ownership information as part of their licensing processes. In 2019, the Ministry of Energy and Mineral Resources signed an agreement with the Ministry of Law and Human Rights to share and integrate their beneficial ownership database systems, which is still a work in progress (footnote 57).

There is an ongoing debate in Indonesia on whether the beneficial ownership information should be made available to the public and whether it should be accessible free of charge. It is argued that the current fee charged to access the registry significantly hinders the process of ensuring accountability and transparency, which is the entire purpose of establishing a beneficial ownership register. The National Strategy for Corruption Prevention (Stranas PK), coordinated by the Indonesian Corruption Eradication Commission, has set a target for beneficial ownership data disclosure by 2022. The country also faces challenges in data verification and accuracy; in ensuring the availability of complete, accurate, and up-to-date beneficial ownership information; and in identifying PEPs as beneficial owners in the central registry.

As a next step, it has been identified that interagency collaboration on beneficial ownership information, including the establishment of integrated beneficial ownership data management systems, needs to be improved to support the development of a robust verification system. Awareness raising and capacity-building activities with companies are also needed to provide guidance on reporting beneficial ownership data. Indonesia is also currently working to promote the use of beneficial ownership data for handling criminal cases, licensing, and public procurement.

C. Kazakhstan

In December 2017, Kazakhstan established the new Code on Subsoil and Subsoil Use. This Code requires mining companies to disclose their beneficial ownership information to the Ministry of Industry and Infrastructure Development (MIID) as a part of the licensing process. Similarly, oil and gas companies are required, as a part of the licensing process, to disclose their beneficial ownership information to the Ministry of Energy.[60]

---

[60]   The Code references a separate order of the Ministry of Energy dated 23 May 2018 (No. 203). In line with this order, the subsoil users for hydrocarbons and uranium mining have to provide the following information on beneficiaries to the Ministry of Energy annually: (i) data on legal entities directly controlling the subsoil user (full name of the direct shareholder and proportion or percentage of the ownership, jurisdiction of registration, registration number); (ii) list of legal entities, indirectly controlling the subsoil user; and (iii) data on individual beneficiaries (surname, first name, and patronymic of the individual; date of birth; individual ID number; citizenship; nationality; living address; correspondence address; job position [in case of a politically significant person]).

The term beneficial owner is not specifically defined in the Code, except for requiring the disclosure of individuals who "directly or indirectly control the applicant" who is applying for the license.[61] The Code does not clearly specify the information that should be collected on beneficial owners when subsoil users apply for a license. However, this appears to be the same information required to be reported on individuals when there is a change in the composition of individuals who directly or indirectly control the subsoil user.[62] This information includes "surname, first name and patronymic (if specified in the identity document), place of residence, citizenship, and information on the identity documents."[63]

If a state-owned enterprise directly or indirectly controls the subsoil user, it is required to disclose the name and location of the state body to which it is accountable.[64] The disclosure of beneficial owners is already in effect in Kazakhstan for the mining sector, and the data is available in an Excel sheet from the MIID website. There is no information available on the collection by the Ministry of Energy of the beneficial ownership data of oil and gas companies, or the availability of that data.

In June 2019, the MIID disclosed beneficial ownership data for the first time on its website. The data includes the names of beneficial owners and their level of ownership. The data only covers all licenses awarded since October 2018 and is available in an Excel sheet.[65] There is also a lack of clear information on the data verification mechanisms used by the MIID to ensure that the beneficial ownership information reported by entities is complete, accurate, and updated on a timely basis.

The Code on Subsoil and Subsoil Use provides for sanctions if a license is obtained by deliberately submitting false information to relevant authorities (i.e., the MIID and the Ministry of Energy) which influence the decision to issue the license.[66] However, it is not clear whether this also applies to submitting false beneficial ownership information. The Code on Administrative Violations also contains penalties in the form of a fine (nearly $150.00) in the event of a violation of the terms and procedures for reporting by subsoil users,[67] which could also be interpreted as including violations relating to reporting beneficial ownership information. Nonetheless, the sanctions and penalties imposed by the Code do not appear to be dissuasive or proportionate.

---

[61] Code on Subsoil and Subsoil Use, 2017. Article 40 (3).
[62] According to Article 47 of the Code, in case of any change in the control composition, the subsoil user is required to notify the relevant state authority about individuals and legal entities that gained or "lost control" over it within 30 days from the date of such change.
[63] Footnote 61, Article 47.
[64] Footnote 61, Article 47(2).
[65] EITI Kazakhstan (updated information provided during consultation meetings). See also Ministry of Industry and Infrastructural Development of the Republic of Kazakhstan. https://www.gov.kz/memleket/entities/ miid/documents/2?activities=10724&lang=en (accessed 6 June 2022).
[66] Footnote 61, Article 34 (1).
[67] Article 349 (fine is 20 monthly calculation indices, where 1 month calculation index is about $7).

As a next step, it has been identified that intergovernmental collaboration on beneficial ownership information needs to be improved to support the development of a robust verification system, to ensure comprehensive beneficial ownership disclosures for the mining sector, and to develop a beneficial ownership register for oil and gas companies that is accessible to the public. Capacity-building activities with companies are also needed to provide guidance on reporting beneficial ownership data.

D. Kyrgyz Republic

In May 2018, the Kyrgyz Republic adopted the Subsoil Law, which requires companies, excluding publicly listed companies, to disclose their beneficial owners when they apply for or hold an extractives license. The term beneficial owners, as defined under Article 4 of the Subsoil Law, covers three categories of direct or indirect ownership or control—shares, votes, and power to appoint board members. The definition does not extend to "other means of control" (e.g., informal control or control via nominees). The threshold of 10% ownership is used in the Subsoil Law to determine beneficial ownership, and for beneficial ownership disclosures.

The State Committee on Industry, Energy and Subsoil Use (SCIESU) has been mandated under the Subsoil Law to collect and publicly disclose beneficial ownership information. The law also incorporates sanctions and penalties for non-compliance with beneficial ownership disclosure requirements. In order to implement the beneficial ownership register, in August 2018, the country signed a memorandum of understanding with Open Ownership regarding establishing a publicly accessible register of beneficial ownership linked to extractives licenses that is freely accessible online and that produces high-quality beneficial ownership data aligned with the BODS.

In September 2019, the Kyrgyz Republic approved the beneficial ownership bylaws, which were submitted to the government for approval by the SCIESU. The Regulations on Licensing of Subsoil Use Rights, as amended in September 2020, incorporate further provisions on (i) the beneficial ownership information that must be disclosed to the SCIESU (including the disclosure of beneficial owners who are regarded as PEPs), (ii) the procedure for disclosing beneficial ownership information, (iii) the public disclosure of beneficial ownership information on the SCIESU website, and (iv) the timescale (of 60 calendar days) for updating the beneficial ownership information in the event of any changes. However, beneficial ownership information has not yet been made available to the public by the SCIESU.

In 2022, the SCIESU was reorganized into the Department of Geology and Subsoil Use under the Ministry of Natural Resources, Ecology and Technical Supervision of the Kyrgyz Republic. The Department of Geology and Subsoil Use is currently looking for funding to reform its existing license register to include beneficial ownership information. However, the department still collects information on beneficial ownership in hard copy, as a part of the licensing procedures. The information is maintained in the archive of the license department of the Ministry of Natural Resources, Ecology, and Technical Supervision. The Kyrgyz Republic is currently developing the Mining Code, which also incorporates the beneficial ownership disclosure provisions contained within the Subsoil Law.

The Kyrgyz Republic has a Unified State Register of Legal Entities, maintained by the Ministry of Justice, who is responsible for registering all legal entities in the country. The register contains basic ownership information for legal entities. To ensure effective implementation of the national anti-money laundering/combating the financing of terrorism (AML/CFT) law, in 2018, the Kyrgyz Republic approved regulations regarding the establishment of an electronic database containing information on beneficial owners (Annex 8 to Resolution No. 606).[68] No further information is available on the establishment of such an electronic database of beneficial ownership information.

However, during the consultation meetings, it was mentioned that the beneficial ownership information for about 30% of extractives sector companies is publicly available through the Unified State Register of Legal Entities. Nevertheless, there are no mechanisms in place to verify the accuracy and currency of the legal ownership or beneficial ownership information submitted to the Ministry of Justice by companies,[69] except in as much as the FIU is obliged to ensure that the information contained in the database is kept up-to-date (footnote 68). No timeline is provided for updating the beneficial ownership information contained in the database.

The Kyrgyz Republic still faces challenges in ensuring the completeness, accuracy, and availability of up-to-date beneficial ownership information on legal entities, and in establishing effective mechanisms to make information available to the public. There are limited technical resources and digital infrastructure for electronically collecting and processing all the beneficial ownership data collected in paper format from extractives sector companies by the Department of Geology and Subsoil Use. There is also a lack of clarity on the interaction and interoperability between the beneficial ownership databases maintained respectively by the Department of Geology and Subsoil Use and the Ministry of Justice.

As a next step, the country needs to amend its legal and/or regulatory framework to ensure that all the required beneficial ownership information, including the PEP status, is collected and is made available to the public. The country also needs to adopt and implement effective data collection and verification mechanisms to ensure the accuracy and availability of up-to-date beneficial ownership information within the register. The intergovernmental collaboration on beneficial ownership information needs to be improved to support the development of a robust verification system and to develop a beneficial ownership register that is accessible to the public.

---

68   EAG. 2019. *Kyrgyz Republic: Second Enhanced Follow-Up Report.* 29 November. p. 11.
69   EAG. 2018. *Mutual Evaluation of Kyrgyz Republic.* p. 109.

E. Mongolia

Beneficial ownership transparency (BOT) is one of the top priorities of the government's agenda in Mongolia. The General Authority for Intellectual Property and State Registration (GAIPSR) provides information on the establishment and types of legal persons in Mongolia. Under the General Law on State Registration 2018, all legal entities in Mongolia are obliged to disclose their basic legal ownership information to the GAIPSR.[70] Under Article 10.1.14 of the General Law on State Registration 2018, legal entities holding a mining license are required to disclose their beneficial ownership information to the GAIPSR, including the share, interest, and voting right of the beneficial owner(s). There is, however, no specific reporting requirement for foreign PEP beneficial owners.[71]

The GAIPSR maintains a database with the details of each legal person registered in Mongolia, both in physical and electronic form.[72] Nonetheless, the beneficial ownership information of legal entities is not yet accessible to the public, although basic information on companies is publicly available. In 2021, Mongolia enacted a law on public information which will allow the public to access the beneficial ownership data, among other data, of companies from all sectors. The law became effective on 1 May 2022, but the mechanism for the public to access such beneficial ownership data has to be decided as the country formulates implementing rules and regulations for the law. The government has also passed a new law on the protection of personal data (data privacy), which also took effect on 1 May 2022.

To ensure that the beneficial ownership information provided to the GAIPSR is complete and accurate, provisions have been incorporated into the General Law on State Registration. The law imposes an obligation on persons in charge of registering legal entities, or registering amendments to existing legal persons, to disclose true and accurate information to the GAIPSR, including the required beneficial ownership information (footnote 70). Additionally, the GAIPSR is required to analyze and confirm the veracity and correctness of the data provided for registration, and to register it in the database after verification (footnote 70). However, it is not clear how this is being done in practice by the GAIPSR.

Furthermore, it should be noted that while the General Law on State Registration 2018 ensures uniformity with the Law on Combating Money Laundering and Terrorism Financing 2013, it does not indicate any threshold in its definition of beneficial owner(s). Nonetheless, the threshold of 33% is set for beneficial ownership

---

[70] APG. 2019. *2nd Follow-Up Report: Mutual Evaluation of Mongolia* October. p. 10.
[71] Barron, M. et al. 2021. *Beneficial Ownership in Mongolia: A Way Forward.* LTRC. September. p. 24; Multi-Stakeholder Group (MSG) has published a list of companies holding extractives licenses in Mongolia that are subsidiaries of companies publicly listed on foreign stock exchanges, however, they do not have specific references or linkages to their statutory filings for their respective stock exchanges.
[72] APG. 2017. *Anti-Money Laundering and Countering Terrorist Financing Measures: Mutual Evaluation of Mongolia.* September. p. 126.

reporting of legal entities in the beneficial ownership information registration form.[73] On the other hand, EITI-Mongolia discloses beneficial ownership data for extractives companies at a lower threshold (5%), reported through its eReporting platform. Such inconsistencies in the beneficial ownership threshold might result in some inconsistencies and confusion in the beneficial ownership disclosures made by different types of companies and sectors. Moreover, there is also a lack of uniformity about how the term "beneficial owner(s)" is defined by Mongolia's General Law on Taxation 2019 and Banking Law 2010, including the indicated threshold of 30% and 5%, respectively.[74]

The Law on Infringement punishes both failing to give correct and truthful information to the GAIPSR when registering a legal person and violating the legal requirements of Mongolia's AML/CFT law involving identifying beneficial owners.[75]

Despite these developments toward BOT, there are challenges that remain in Mongolia, including the lack of digitalization of beneficial ownership information, the need to design and implement a public beneficial ownership register, the need to ensure efficient and effective collection and verification of beneficial ownership information, and the interaction between the beneficial ownership register and other available registers (such as the register for asset declarations of public officials). Available reports note that the GAIPSR has embarked on the digitalization of beneficial ownership data, and that wider digitalization of government services is a priority.

F. Papua New Guinea

Papua New Guinea (PNG) has shown its commitment to beneficial ownership disclosure by enacting the AML/CFT Act 2015 (No. 20 of 2015), the PNG Roadmap for beneficial ownership disclosure, the National Policy for Transparency and Accountability in the Extractives Sector, and the National Action Plan on Promotion of Open Governance (2018–2020).

Companies engaged in the extractives sector are required to reveal their beneficial owners under PNG's implementation of the EITI standard. In compliance with the international standards, the PNG-EITI Multi-Stakeholder Group (MSG) defines "beneficial owner(s)" as "the natural person(s) who ultimately control(s) or own(s) the legal entity, whether such ownership or control is direct or indirect."[76] A materiality threshold of 5% has been set to determine beneficial ownership, but the definition also takes into consideration other means of exercising significant control or influence (footnote 76).

---

[73]   Footnote 71, p. 9.
[74]   Footnote 71, pp. 9–10.
[75]   Footnote 70, p. 10.
[76]   BDO Consulting. 2020. *Final Report: BO Study—Papua New Guinea.* December. p. 6. http://www.pngeiti.org.
        pg/wp-content/uploads/2020/12/BDO_PNG-EITI-BO-Report-Final-version-20-12-20.pdf.

PEPs are also included within the PNG-EITI definition of beneficial ownership; and they are required to be reported if they own a single share or single voting right or more in a legal entity, or if they otherwise exercise ultimate control or influence (footnote 76). On the other hand, Article 5 of the Anti-Money Laundering and Counter Terrorist Financing Act 2015 (No. 20 of 2015) of PNG defines "beneficial owner" as "a natural person who – (a) has ultimate control, directly or indirectly, of a customer; or (b) ultimately owns, directly or indirectly, the customer."[77] There is no indication of the existence of any threshold in this definition, and it appears to be mainly focused on the identification of beneficial owners by financial institutions and designated nonfinancial businesses and professions (DNFBPs).

Using the beneficial ownership disclosure template approved by the PNG-EITI MSG, all legal companies that apply for or hold a participation interest in exploration and production contracts or licenses in the oil, gas, and mining sectors are invited to submit their beneficial ownership information. The PNG-EITI MSG has also recently approved new beneficial ownership guidelines, which include a data assurance procedure. Nonetheless, one of the recent studies on beneficial ownership regime in PNG reveals that only 21 of PNG's 145 extractives companies have turned in their beneficial ownership declarations.[78] Twenty of these 21 companies were more than 95% owned subsidiaries of publicly traded companies (footnote 77). None of the reported beneficial owners were identified as PEPs by the corporate entities (footnote 77).

Despite its commitments to BOT under various pieces of legislation and international initiatives, PNG does not currently have a legal framework for beneficial ownership disclosure or a mandatory beneficial ownership disclosure regime, which is one of the major hindrances to collecting and verifying beneficial ownership data. During the consultation meeting, it was highlighted that PNG's Investment Promotion Authority, the company regulator, is currently receiving technical assistance through an ADB-funded project for developing the legal framework for beneficial ownership disclosure by introducing the necessary reforms in the company law. It is anticipated that PNG will implement the collection of beneficial ownership data through the Investment Promotion Authority online system, which is used for the existing company register.

As a next step, PNG needs to receive substantial institutional guidance on, and to study examples of, emerging international good practices in developing and implementing a legal and regulatory framework for beneficial ownership disclosure. Increased political commitment is needed to drive legislative and policy reforms on BOT. There are also anticipated resource and capacity constraints to maintaining the beneficial ownership register and collecting data from multilayered companies. PNG also needs capacity-building support in raising awareness about the concept of beneficial ownership in the country.[79]

---

[77]   Government of Papua New Guinea. Anti-Money Laundering and Counter Terrorist Financing Act 2015 (No. 20 of 2015) Article 5.
[78]   Footnote 77, p. 4.
[79]   Footnote 77, p. 5.

G. Philippines

In 2018, the Philippines' Securities and Exchange Commission (SEC) issued Memorandum Circular No. 17, series of 2018, requiring all SEC-registered stock and non-stock domestic corporations, including extractives industry companies, to report their beneficial ownership information to the SEC through their annual filing of General Information Sheets with the SEC. The beneficial ownership information is required to be reported annually, within 30 calendar days from the date of the annual meeting of stockholders,[80] or within 7 working days of a change in the beneficial ownership information.[81]

In 2019, a new Memorandum Circular No. 15, series of 2019, was issued by the SEC, which amended Memorandum Circular No. 17, series of 2018, further strengthening the BOT and beneficial ownership disclosure requirements in the Philippines. The beneficial ownership information required to be reported under the Memorandum Circular No. 15, series of 2019, includes "the beneficial owner's complete name, specific residential address, date of birth, nationality, and tax identification number, and the percentage of ownership, if applicable."[82]

In 2020, the SEC issued another Memorandum Circular No. 30, series of 2020, requiring all SEC-registered foreign corporations to disclose their beneficial owners to the SEC through annual General Information Sheets. In January 2021, the SEC also issued guidelines to corporate entities on promoting BOT.[83]

If a corporation fails to disclose beneficial ownership information, the SEC has the power to impose financial penalties on it, as well as on its directors, trustees, and other senior managing officials.[84] Under Memorandum Circular No. 15, series of 2019, the competent authorities shall be given access to the beneficial ownership information for law enforcement and other lawful purposes (e.g., compliance with court orders). However, the information is not made publicly available. Due to data privacy concerns, until recently, information on beneficial owners was not even reported under the EITI standard. However, recently, some extractives companies have disclosed their beneficial ownership information and allowed for its publication through the sixth and seventh EITI reports. The information published in these reports is based on company declarations to the SEC and/or PH-EITI, and on company submissions to PH-EITI in September 2020.

As a next step, the Philippines should consider introducing the necessary legal and regulatory reforms to provide public access to beneficial ownership information, and incorporating effective verification mechanisms to ensure the accuracy and

---

80   General Information Sheet (GIS), Memorandum Circular No. 17, Series of 2018.
81   Section 5, Memorandum Circular No. 17, Series of 2018.
82   Section 3, Memorandum Circular No. 15, Series of 2019.
83   SEC. 2021. *Guidelines in Preventing the Misuse of Corporations for Illicit Activities through Measures Designed to Promote Transparency of Beneficial Ownership (BO Transparency Guidelines)*. MC No. 01 s. 2021. https://www.sec.gov.ph/mc-2021/mc-no-01-s-2021/.
84   Section 11, Memorandum Circular No. 15, Series of 2019.

availability of up-to-date beneficial ownership information in the register. Capacity-building and awareness-raising activities on beneficial ownership should also be conducted. The definition of beneficial owners also needs to be harmonized across the country's legal and regulatory framework.

H. Tajikistan

All legal entities doing business in Tajikistan must be included in the Unified State Register, which provides basic information about legal entities, and is accessible and free of charge, via the Tax Committee's website maintained by the Government of Tajikistan.[85] In 2019, Tajikistan introduced amendments to the Law on State Registration of Legal Entities and Individual Entrepreneurs, which requires the disclosure of beneficial ownership information by legal entities when registering for business activities in Tajikistan. The beneficial ownership information required to be disclosed by legal entities includes the legal name, surname, name, and patronymic of the beneficial owner, and his or her location, to be accompanied by the identity document of each beneficial owner.[86] However, this information on beneficial ownership is not publicly available.

In December 2021, Tajikistan EITI launched a Beneficial Ownership portal, which discloses available information from the Tax Committee. The portal is available in three languages and covers data from 41 extractives companies engaged in exploration, oil, gas, and mining which had valid licenses in 2021. The information provided in the portal includes information about the legal owners, and, where available, information about the beneficial owners, the level of ownership, postal address, links to the stock exchange, and how PEPs are identified. In practice, however, none of the companies disclose the PEP status. The portal neither mentions the definition of beneficial ownership used for the disclosure, nor does it comment on verification procedures. Several companies disclose foreign states as their beneficial owners. According to the Tax Committee, there is no regulation in place to enable regular updating of the beneficial ownership information.

As a next step, Tajikistan should consider (i) introducing the necessary legal and regulatory reforms to ensure that all the relevant information on beneficial owners is collected (i.e., increasing the granularity and scope of beneficial ownership disclosures); (ii) establishing effective data collection and verification mechanisms to ensure the completeness, accuracy, and availability of up-to-date beneficial ownership information in the register; (iii) making the beneficial ownership information available to the public; and (iv)) conducting capacity-building and awareness-raising activities on beneficial ownership reporting.

---

[85]   EAG. 2018. *Mutual Evaluation Report of the Republic of Tajikistan.* p. 96.
[86]   Law on State Registration of Legal Entities and Individual Entrepreneurs, 2009. Article 11(1).

I. Timor-Leste

In Timor-Leste, the lack of legislation and clear policies on beneficial ownership poses a challenge to collecting beneficial ownership data.[87] In the extractives sector, companies operating in the country are mainly international oil companies that are not registered in Timor-Leste but rather are the subsidiaries of companies publicly listed on the stock exchange.[88] For such companies, it is anticipated that the source and details regarding the ownership structure are already public. Legal policies and practices regarding BOT and beneficial ownership disclosure are still only partial (footnote 88).

The country clearly needs a high-level commitment to drive forward reforms on ensuring BOT, and more capacity building and technical assistance in regard to developing the necessary legal and regulatory framework, including determining the granularity and scope of beneficial ownership disclosures. Timor-Leste's EITI MSG has started working in this direction, and in 2019, it approved the definition of beneficial owner(s) and PEPs (footnote 88).

---

[87]   Please note that due to the lack of availability of up-to-date information on BOT in Timor-Leste, the information in this section has been extracted mainly from EITI. 2019. *Beneficial Ownership in Asia*. Oslo. February. p. 6. https://eiti.org/sites/default/files/attachments/english_bo_in_asia.pdf.

[88]   EITI Timor-Leste. 2019. *2019 Reconciliation Report*. pp. 102–104. https://tleiti.mpm.gov.tl/wp-content/uploads/2022/03/2019-TL_EITI-Report.pdf.

V. Common Challenges, Best Practices, and Key Considerations

Having analyzed the selected countries' existing legal and regulatory framework, and their systems and mechanisms for BOT, this study identifies and highlights in this section some of the common issues and challenges faced by these countries, as well as other countries in the Asia and Pacific region, in regard to ensuring BOT for corporate entities. While highlighting these challenges, this section also discusses some of the best practices worldwide in regard to ensuring BOT. Finally, the section also provides practical guidance and actionable recommendations for countries to address these challenges, which can inform further discussions at the country level on ensuring the availability of adequate, accurate, and up-to-date information on beneficial owners.

A. Legal and Regulatory Framework

To ensure BOT and compliance with international standards (including the FATF Recommendations, the EITI standard, the Global Forum, and the UNCAC), some countries may need to introduce legislative and regulatory reforms. In a few countries, it will be possible to build on existing laws on combating corruption, money laundering, and terrorist financing, which already require beneficial ownership disclosures.

In other countries, new legislation might be required so that the government can gather the crucial beneficial ownership data and oblige the corporate entities to collect, maintain, and disclose the beneficial ownership information to the relevant authorities, including within the central register, if established. In this regard, the first step for all countries is to conduct a legal gap analysis of their current laws and/or regulations to determine the necessary reforms and to agree on the legislation and/or regulations that need to be amended or newly drafted. For the purposes of this exercise, the countries need to consider and analyze a range of laws and regulations that relate to beneficial ownership, including, for instance, company law, partnership law, AML/CFT law, anticorruption law, and extractives sector laws, to ensure that all the relevant legislation and related bylaws are harmonized in the long term.

Some of the common themes that countries need to analyze and consider at the legal and policy level include the following:

Incorporating Explicit Obligations on Beneficial Ownership Disclosure

Some of the countries selected for this study (for instance, PNG) have experienced difficulties in persuading companies to report and publicly disclose beneficial ownership data, especially where there is no legal obligation to disclose this information. In this regard, one very basic (yet significant) amendment to the relevant laws and/or regulations is to incorporate provisions imposing a legal obligation on companies to obtain and disclose beneficial ownership data.

One of the major policy considerations is for countries to determine whether such an obligation to obtain and disclose the required beneficial ownership information should be incorporated into new stand-alone legislation, or whether existing laws, such as the company law or the AML/CFT law, should be amended to incorporate such an obligation. At the international level, different approaches have been taken by different jurisdictions. For instance, in the United Kingdom (UK), this obligation has been incorporated into the existing Companies Act 2006, by making the necessary amendments.

Similarly, in Armenia, the Law on State Registration of Legal Entities has imposed on legal entities the obligations to (i) carry out regular proper checks and study, not less than once a year, on their beneficial owner(s) and to keep all the relevant documents; (ii) make inquiries of persons who are suspected of being beneficial owner(s), as well as of the participants of the legal entity or the representatives of the participating legal entities, who may possess information on the beneficial owner(s) of the legal entity; and (iii) submit a declaration on its beneficial owner(s) to the Agency of the State Register of Legal Entities based on the results of their beneficial ownership checks and study (footnote 44). Similar approaches have also been adopted by other countries such as Denmark, Tajikistan, and India.

On the other hand, there are countries, such as Austria, Indonesia, Ukraine, Tunisia, and Ghana, where new legislation on a beneficial ownership register has been enacted, which imposes a beneficial ownership disclosure requirement on corporate entities. In a few countries that initially have only imposed the beneficial ownership disclosure requirements on the extractive industries, the relevant beneficial ownership disclosure requirements have been incorporated into the extractives sector legislation, which has either been developed and/or amended accordingly—for instance, in the Kyrgyz Republic and Kazakhstan.

However, it should be emphasized that whichever approach countries prefer to take, depending upon their legal system and BOT policy goals, it is important to ensure that all the relevant laws and/or regulations are amended accordingly to ensure certainty and uniformity. For instance, if the new legislation on a beneficial ownership register is enacted, the relevant provisions in the company law, trust law, AML/CFT law, law related to the extractive industries, and any other legislation and/or regulations should also be amended accordingly.

To ensure that all the relevant laws and regulations related to BOT have been analyzed and a uniform approach has been taken to enhance BOT, this study recommends the formation of a working group consisting of all relevant agencies and authorities responsible for beneficial ownership-related matters (e.g., tax authority, FIU, anticorruption agency, extractives sector agencies). Such working group will identify, propose, and implement the necessary beneficial ownership reforms to avoid fragmented or contradictory regulations. Countries should also consider designating a lead authority or agency to coordinate and lead the work of interagency working group on beneficial ownership reforms.

Important Considerations
• Clearly incorporate the beneficial ownership disclosure requirements in the relevant legislation—whether in a stand-alone law on beneficial ownership register or in existing laws, depending on the country's legal system and BOT policy goals. • Ensure that all relevant pieces of legislations and/or regulations are amended accordingly to ensure certainty and uniformity in the approach. • Establish an interagency working group, with a clearly designated lead coordinating authority or agency, who will conduct a legal gap analysis on BOT requirements as well as propose and implement the necessary beneficial ownership reforms.

Establishing a Single, Unified, and Robust Definition of "Beneficial Owner(s)"

The FATF defines "beneficial owners" as "the natural person(s) who ultimately owns or controls a customer and/or the natural person on whose behalf a transaction is being conducted. It also includes those persons who exercise ultimate effective control over a legal person or arrangement."[89] It further clarifies that the reference to "ultimately owns or controls" and "ultimate effective control" in the FATF definition refers to "situations in which ownership/control is exercised through a chain of ownership or by means of control other than direct control" (footnote 11). In other words, the beneficial owner is the person or persons who benefit(s) from or exercise(s) control, either directly or indirectly, over a legal person. The definition of beneficial owners as provided by other international standards, including the Global Forum, the EITI,[90] and the UNCAC, does not differ from that of the FATF Recommendations and includes within its scope both ownership and control interests.

At the country level, the definitions of the term beneficial owner are usually outlined in different legal instruments (e.g., AML/CFT law, extractives sector-related laws, tax law). In most countries, the definition of beneficial owner(s) extends to cover both ownership and controlling interests, as required by international standards.

---

[89] Footnote 11, p. 119.
[90] Requirement 2.5 of the EITI standard specifies that a beneficial owner is the "natural person(s) who directly or indirectly ultimately owns or controls the corporate entity."

However, the meaning of control and related thresholds varies among countries, as well as among different legal instruments within a country. For instance, in the Kyrgyz Republic, the meaning of "control" is limited to "direct or indirect appointment and/or recall of the members of governing bodies." It does not extend to "other means of control" or exercising "ultimate effective control," as provided by the FATF Recommendations.

Similarly, on thresholds, Mongolia defines beneficial owners differently and uses different thresholds in its General Law on Taxation 2019 (30%), Banking Law 2010 (10%), beneficial ownership disclosure forms under the 2018 General Law on State Registration (33%), and EITI-Mongolia MSG definition (5%).[91] This lack of a single, unified definition, with a restricted meaning of control and varying thresholds under different legal instruments, has usually been identified as a significant loophole in the legal and regulatory framework of jurisdictions, which might result in inadequate beneficial ownership information, as well as significant confusion and misunderstanding among the reporting entities, competent authorities, and the legal persons as to their beneficial ownership disclosure requirements. Consequently, it would be difficult for legal persons and reporting entities to collect the relevant beneficial ownership information, as well as for countries to produce corresponding forms for data collection for beneficial ownership registers.

At the international level, no clear consensus has emerged so far over the level at which the threshold for determining beneficial ownership should be set. The FATF Recommendations do not mandate a threshold for determining a controlling participation by legal persons. Countries are given the discretion to set their own threshold, considering the level of risks (i.e., money laundering, terrorist financing) facing the legal persons in their jurisdiction. However, the FATF Interpretive Note to Recommendation 24,[92] its 2014 guidance on the transparency of legal persons,[93] and its assessment process appear to uphold a threshold of 25% as acceptable.[94] As a result, the majority of countries, while complying with the example provided in the FATF Guidance and Interpretive Note to Recommendation 24, apply the threshold of "25%" or "more than 25%,"[95] and this threshold is also incorporated in the beneficial ownership definitions of other leading international policy instruments, such as the Common Reporting Standard for AEOI and the EU Fifth AML Directive.[96]

---

[91] Footnote 71, p. 9.
[92] Footnote 71, p. 65.
[93] FATF. 2014. *Transparency and Beneficial Ownership*. Paris. October. https://www.fatf-gafi.org/media/fatf/documents/reports/Guidance-transparency-beneficial-ownership.pdf.
[94] Footnote 7, p. 14.
[95] These include, for instance, Austria, Belgium, Bulgaria, Croatia, Cyprus, Czech Republic, Denmark, Estonia, Finland, France, Germany, Greece, Indonesia, Ireland, Italy, Latvia, Lithuania, Luxembourg, Malta, the Netherlands, Portugal, Romania, Slovakia, Spain, Sweden, Switzerland, Ukraine, and the United Kingdom.
[96] Directive (EU) 2018/843 of the European Parliament and of the Council of 30 May 2018 amending Directive (EU) 2015/849 on the prevention of the use of the financial system for the purposes of money laundering or terrorist financing, and amending Directives 2009/138/EC and 2013/36/EU (hereinafter referred to as the EU 5th AML Directive).

However, many countries and initiatives have opted for lower thresholds for identifying a beneficial owner or a person who is considered to have a controlling interest, considering that the higher threshold might leave relevant beneficial owners outside the scope of disclosures. For example, Argentina, Armenia, the Dominican Republic, the Philippines, and Tunisia use a threshold of 20%; Uruguay, 15%; Barbados, the Bahamas, Belize, and Jersey, 10%; and Colombia and Sri Lanka, 5%. The EITI and Open Ownership also strongly advocate for, and promote the adoption of, a lower threshold for identifying beneficial owners.[97]

To determine the threshold level appropriate for a country to establish an effective beneficial ownership disclosure regime, the country must first examine the policy goals behind their BOT regime and then adopt a risk-based approach to effectively meet their specific policy goals.[98] For a majority of countries, the policy goals include, for instance, tackling corruption, money laundering, terrorist financing, and tax evasion, or supporting economic activity by lowering the likelihood of fraud and the cost of due diligence. High thresholds leave a disclosure regime vulnerable to loopholes, while lower thresholds might unnecessarily increase the reporting burden on legal persons and are likely to require more state investment in communicating and explaining how to comply with the disclosure requirements.

Additionally, the lower the threshold is set, the more challenging it is for legal persons to get updated with the accurate identification of beneficial owners. On the other hand, there is also an argument made by Elizabeth Fiona Alpe that lower thresholds would be useful in capturing the necessary information on legal persons with complex ownership and control structures—which might be lesser in number, but where the problem often lies.[99] E. F. Alpe highlighted that such an approach would not necessarily be an issue for the majority of companies with simple ownership structures, but it could be utilized in generating useful data (footnote 99).

---

[97] See Open Ownership. 2020. *Beneficial Ownership in Law: Definitions*. Policy Briefing. October. https://openownershiporgprod-1b54.kxcdn.com/media/documents/oo-briefing-bo-in-law-definitions-and-thresholds-2020-10.pdf; and Ime, F. and L. Russell-Prywata. 2022. Beneficial Ownership Transparency and the Fight Against Grand Corruption in Nigeria. *Open Ownership Blog*. 15 February. https://www.openownership.org/en/blog/beneficial-ownership-transparency-and-the-fight-against-grand-corruption-in-nigeria/.

[98] A risk-based approach to AML/CFT, as provided by the FATF under its Recommendation 1, means that countries, competent authorities, and the private sector should identify, assess, and understand the money laundering and terrorist financing risks to which they are exposed and take measures commensurate with those risks to mitigate them effectively. The risk-based approach is crucial to effective implementation of the FATF Recommendations. It allows countries to adopt a more flexible set of measures while adhering to the FATF requirements. By applying preventive measures commensurate with the nature of risks, countries can target their resources more effectively and concentrate their efforts in the most efficient manner.

[99] Alpe, E . F. 2022. *BO Data Verification Mechanisms: Policy, Technical and Practical Considerations*. Presentation made during ADB and EITI Regional Workshop on Advancing Beneficial Ownership Transparency. 21–23 February. See also Open Ownership. 2020. *Beneficial Ownership in Law: Definitions*. Policy Briefing. October. https://openownershiporgprod-1b54.kxcdn.com/media/documents/oo-briefing-bo-in-law-definitions-and-thresholds-2020-10.pdf; and Ime, F. and L. Russell-Prywata. 2022. Beneficial Ownership Transparency and the Fight Against Grand Corruption in Nigeria. *Open Ownership Blog*. 15 February. https://www.openownership.org/en/blog/beneficial-ownership-transparency-and-the-fight-against-grand-corruption-in-nigeria/.

While applying the risk-based approach, it is however possible under some circumstances that countries can apply different thresholds across different sectors of the economy. For example, an economy that is highly dependent on revenues from resource extraction—a sector that is known to be prone to corruption—may apply a lower threshold for extractives sector disclosures than for non-extractives sector legal persons.

In Ghana, for instance, the beneficial ownership disclosure threshold for high-risk sectors, such as extractives, banking, insurance, and gaming, is 5%, whereas it is 20% for companies in other sectors.[100] In such cases, however, care should be taken to avoid creating a loophole where companies can choose which disclosure regime they fall under. To mitigate this risk, a clear definition of each economic sector to which a particular threshold applies is recommended. Mechanisms should also be in place for the periodic review of threshold(s) by country authorities to ensure that the level selected is appropriate and to enable the country to achieve the policy goals connected with beneficial ownership disclosures.

Important Considerations

- Ensure that the definition of beneficial owner(s) includes within its scope both direct and indirect ownership and controlling interests, including natural person(s) who ultimately own(s) or control(s) or exercise(s) ultimate effective control over legal entities or arrangements.
- Adopt a single, unified, and robust definition of beneficial ownership in the primary legislation—with potential variations in thresholds for disclosure for the extractives sector and for non-extractives sectors—to minimize loopholes and to make it easier to produce corresponding forms for data collection.

Clarity on the Scope of Legal Entities to Be Covered by Beneficial Ownership Disclosure Rules

In line with the international AML/CFT standards, financial institutions and DNFBPs are required to identify and take reasonable steps to identify the beneficial owner(s) of all their customers, including all types of legal persons and legal arrangements, as a part of their customer due diligence (CDD) process.[101] However, in the case of the registry approach, there arises an issue wherein legal entities should be covered within the scope of the beneficial ownership disclosure regime. In this case, it is important that the legislation clearly specifies the entities responsible for the disclosure of their beneficial ownership information within the register and who, on behalf of an entity, is responsible for reporting such information.

---

[100] Ime, F., and L. Russell-Prywata. 2022. Beneficial Ownership Transparency and the Fight Against Grand Corruption in Nigeria. *Open Ownership Blog*. 15 February. https://www.openownership.org/en/blog/beneficial-ownership-transparency-and-the-fight-against-grand-corruption-in-nigeria/.

[101] Footnote 11, Recommendation 10; See definition of "relevant entities and arrangements" in Global Forum. 2016. *Exchange of Information on Request: Handbook for Peer Reviews 2016–2020—2016 Terms of Reference*. Paris: OECD. p. 19; The EOIR standard states that "relevant Entities and Arrangements" includes (i) a company, foundation, Anstalt, and any similar structure; (ii) a partnership or other body of persons; (iii) a trust or similar arrangement; (iv) a collective investment fund or scheme; (v) any person holding assets in a fiduciary capacity; and (vi) any other entity or arrangement deemed relevant in the case of the specific jurisdiction assessed.

Typically, legal entities, such as companies and limited liability partnerships, are obliged to disclose their beneficial ownership information. Some jurisdictions also require other types of legal entities and legal arrangements to disclose their beneficial ownership information—for instance, partnerships in Indonesia and the Netherlands; limited partnerships in Indonesia and the UK; trusts, foundations, and associations in Austria, Belgium, and Denmark; and non-profit organizations in Albania, Belgium, Indonesia, and Ukraine. A few jurisdictions, such as France, Indonesia, Malaysia, and Zambia, also distinguish between corporations incorporated in the country and those incorporated elsewhere when it comes to beneficial ownership disclosure.[102]

Some countries also provide exemptions for beneficial ownership disclosure to certain legal entities. Publicly listed companies (e.g., in Malaysia and France) and political parties, art unions, lawyers' associations, chambers of commerce and industry, and local self-government entities (as in Albania and Ukraine) are a few examples of exempt entities. Companies listed on regulated markets that are already subject to sufficient disclosure requirements are another example (e.g., in the UK).

While applying a risk-based approach, countries usually determine which corporate entities should fall within the scope of the beneficial ownership disclosure. For instance, the UK did not initially include Scottish Limited Partnerships within the scope of legal entities required to disclose their beneficial ownership information in the central register. However, at some point, based on a risk assessment regarding these types of legal entities, several measures were taken to prevent their misuse for illegal purposes, including extending the beneficial ownership disclosure requirements to Scottish Limited Partnerships and certain general partnerships in Scotland in 2017.[103]

Similarly, a few countries, while applying a risk-based approach, also provide exemptions from the beneficial ownership disclosure requirements to certain legal entities. The most common exempted category is publicly listed companies. It is important to emphasize here that when granting exemption—for instance, in the case of publicly listed companies—countries should not provide blanket exemptions for all companies listed on any stock exchange, since the transparency and disclosure requirements differ widely between stock exchanges, which might hinder BOT measures.[104]

---

[102] It should be noted that the newly revised FATF Recommendation 24 requires countries to ensure that the competent authorities should have access to the necessary beneficial ownership information on foreign legal entities that are incorporated outside their country but have "sufficient links" with the country, which should be determined based on risk. Examples of "sufficiency links," as provided by the Revised FATF Recommendation 24, include, but are not limited to, "when a company has permanent establishment/branch/ agency, has significant business activity or has significant and ongoing business relations with FIs [financial institutions] or DNFBPs, subject to AML/CFT regulation, has significant real estate/other local investment, employs staff, or is a tax resident, in the country."

[103] Footnote 13, pp. 29–30.

[104] This has also been highlighted by E. F. Alpe; See footnote 99.

Listed companies should only be exempted from beneficial ownership disclosure requirements by applying a risk-based approach and only if it is established that adequate and enforced beneficial ownership disclosure requirements exist for the stock exchange(s) on which the company is listed.[105] Such a risk-based approach is commensurate with the FATF standards, which require that countries assess the risk of the misuse of legal persons for money laundering and terrorist financing, and take appropriate measures to prevent their misuse, which includes beneficial ownership disclosure requirements.

Nonetheless, to prevent the misuse of corporate entities for any criminal purposes, this study strongly recommends that countries should include the widest possible range of corporate entities (including foreign legal entities) within the scope of the beneficial ownership disclosure requirements. If any exemptions are to be granted, they should be fully justified based on the risk-based approach. With respect to foreign legal entities, the Interpretive Note to the revised FATF Recommendation 24 now provides that competent authorities should have access in a timely manner to the beneficial ownership and control information of legal persons that have "sufficient links" with their country, if they are not incorporated in the country. Countries are given the discretion to determine and define "sufficient link" based on their risk assessment.

Nonetheless, the Interpretive Note to Recommendation 24 provides a few examples of entities satisfying a sufficiency test: "a company having a permanent establishment/branch/agency, has a significant business activity or a significant and ongoing business relations with financial institutions or DNFBPs, has a significant real estate/other local investment, employs staff, or is a tax resident in a country."[106] To ensure that the beneficial ownership information of such entities is available and accessible to competent authorities in a timely manner, it is thus important for them to be covered within the scope of legal entities that should disclose their beneficial ownership information within the register.

On the question of who should be responsible for reporting the beneficial ownership information on behalf of an entity, different approaches have been adopted by different jurisdictions. Commonly, corporate directors, holders of mining titles or concessions (in Indonesia, Kazakhstan, and the Kyrgyz Republic), and company managers (in Indonesia) are made responsible for reporting beneficial ownership information.[107]

---

[105]   Lord, J., and K. Armstrong. 2020. *Beneficial Ownership Transparency and Listed Companies.* Open Ownership. September. https://openownershiporgprod-1b54.kxcdn.com/media/documents/oo-guidance-technical-note-beneficial-ownership-and-listed-companies-2020-09.pdf.

[106]   The FATF Recommendations 2012. INR 24. p. 91; A similar requirement is also applicable to foreign companies under the EOIR standard, as provided by the Global Forum. 2016. *Exchange of Information on Request: Handbook for Peer Reviews 2016–2020—2016 Terms of Reference.* Paris: OECD. p. 19; It states that where a foreign company has a "sufficient nexus," then the availability of beneficial ownership information is also required to the extent that the company has a relationship with an AML-obligated service provider that is relevant for the purposes of EOIR.

[107]   EITI. 2019. *Legal Approaches to Beneficial Ownership Transparency in EITI Countries.* Oslo. June. p. 3.

In some countries, legal professionals (like in Zambia and Slovakia) and public notaries (such as in Indonesia and Slovakia) are subject to the obligation. This study recommends that the declaring person should either be a member of the senior management team of a legal entity or a DNFBP subject to AML/CFT obligations (for example, a lawyer, accountant, tax advisor, or notary) within the country who can be held accountable by the competent authorities for providing beneficial ownership information to the register, as well as for any other assistance.

Important Considerations

- Ensure that a wide range of legal entities, including foreign entities, subsidiaries, and joint ventures, are included within the scope of the beneficial ownership disclosure requirements for the register.
- Any exemptions for beneficial ownership disclosure requirements given to certain legal entities should be fully justified, considering the level of risk.
- Clearly identify the authorized person(s) responsible for disclosing the beneficial ownership information within the register.

Designated Authority Responsible for Collecting, Maintaining, and Verifying Data

Under the company approach and the existing information approach, as per FATF Recommendation 24, legal entities, financial institutions, and DNFBPs should be required to collect, maintain, and verify (in the case of financial institutions and DNFBPs) beneficial ownership information. However, it is under the registry approach that the issue most arises of who should be responsible, or made responsible, for collecting, maintaining, and verifying the beneficial ownership data or information for corporate entities. This might vary from country to country, depending upon their legal and institutional framework.

To ensure proper implementation and enforcement, legislation should clearly identify the agency (or agencies) in charge of collecting, maintaining, and verifying beneficial ownership information. The recently revised FATF Recommendation 24 provides for the beneficial ownership information to be held by a public authority or body, which could be, for instance, a tax authority, the FIU, the company registry, or the beneficial ownership registry; and the information is not required to be held by a single body only.[108] The EITI standard stipulates that, "where possible, [beneficial ownership] information should be incorporated into existing filings by companies to corporate regulators, stock exchanges, or agencies regulating extractives industries licensing" (footnote 17).

In practice, the agencies responsible for maintaining beneficial ownership data vary across jurisdictions depending on the type of legislation. In the UK, and Zambia, for instance, corporate regulators are identified as the competent authority because the beneficial ownership provisions are included in company legislation.

---

[108]   The FATF Recommendations 2012. INR 24. p. 93.

In Indonesia and Ukraine, the Ministry of Law/Justice, which has the authority to regulate corporations, oversees the beneficial ownership data. Even though the beneficial ownership register in Indonesia is housed by the Ministry of Law, Indonesia's Presidential Regulation on beneficial ownership also lists other authorities with the competence to verify the beneficial ownership data. In the case of sector-specific laws, the extractives sector's regulating ministry (for instance, in the Kyrgyz Republic) is considered the competent authority. Other examples include the tax authorities (in Brazil), the Ministry of Investment and Development (in Kazakhstan), and the central bank (in Uruguay and Costa Rica).

Generally, the approach adopted by a country in designating an authority responsible for collecting and maintaining the beneficial ownership data depends on its legal and institutional framework, including the resource considerations of different agencies. Each approach has its own pros and cons, depending on the country's objectives for BOT. For instance, a sector approach (e.g., in the case of the extractives sector) could be more targeted when it comes to collecting data that detects corruption risks in the issuance of licenses; a company regulator approach, on the other hand, would be beneficial in enabling a wider scope of legal entities to be covered within the beneficial ownership disclosure regime, hence providing greater opportunities for the interoperability of data.[109] A country may decide for more than one agency or authority to obtain and maintain the beneficial ownership data. However, where more than one authority or agency is designated with collecting and maintaining beneficial ownership information (e.g., in Indonesia), it is important to ensure that there is effective cooperation between them. The integration and interoperability of beneficial ownership data and information are also critical for enhancing its quality.

Considering their BOT goals, it is important for countries to clearly identify in their legislation the authority or authorities responsible for collecting and verifying beneficial ownership information, and for enforcing sanctions and/or penalties for violations. Poor identification of the responsible agency and/or mixed responsibilities among multiple agencies may result in gaps in beneficial ownership disclosure and verification, and the enforcement of penalties for violations.

Based on the best practices and lessons learned from other jurisdictions, this study strongly recommends that, when determining the authorities that should be made responsible for the collection, maintenance, and verification of beneficial ownership data, countries should consider the long-term BOT goal. This should involve encompassing all corporate entities within the scope of beneficial ownership disclosure requirements and ensuring the interoperability of beneficial ownership data.

---

[109]   Ordenes, G. 2022. *Beneficial Ownership Data Collection and Disclosure – Policy Considerations*. Presentation made during ADB and EITI Regional Workshop on Advancing Beneficial Ownership Transparency. 21–23 February 2022.

Important Considerations
• Clearly identify the authorities responsible for collecting, maintaining, and verifying the beneficial ownership information. This may include the companies' registrar, the tax authority, or another designated authority, depending on the legal and institutional framework of a country, as well as the national objectives for beneficial ownership transparency.
• If the beneficial ownership data are to be collected and maintained by more than one authority or agency, the legal and regulatory framework should clearly designate the role, responsibilities, and powers of each authority and ensure effective cooperation between the authorities and interoperability of beneficial ownership data.
• Give adequate powers to the designated authorities responsible for collecting, maintaining, and verifying the beneficial ownership data to ensure effective compliance with disclosure requirements.

Treatment of Bearer Shares, Nominee Shareholders, and Nominee Directors

Bearer shares and bearer share warrants can be used to complicate the ownership structure of a legal entity and make it difficult to identify the beneficial owner(s). Any person who has the shares (on paper) at any one time is considered a shareholder or owner of the entity that issues bearer shares. Although dividends are paid against the presentation of paper shares, the beneficial owner's identity is not always made public. Ownership of bearer shares can be changed by simply passing the shares to a new owner. It is very challenging to identify a beneficial owner who controls an entity using bearer shares since it is impossible to know who is currently in possession of the shares at any given moment and because they can be kept anywhere, such as a safe deposit box or a bank.[110]

Considering the risks associated with bearer shares and bearer share warrants, the revised FATF Recommendation 24 requires that "countries do not allow their legal persons to issue new bearer shares or bearer share warrants, and to take measures to prevent the misuse of existing bearer shares and bearer share warrants."[111]

To ensure compliance with the revised FATF Recommendation 24, this study strongly recommends that countries amend their existing laws and regulations to prohibit the issuance of any new bearer shares or bearer share warrants, and to incorporate the necessary measures to prevent the misuse of bearer shares or bearer share warrants for any illegal purposes (e.g., phasing out or immobilizing existing bearer shares).

---

[110]   Footnote 7, p. 5.
[111]   Revised Recommendation 24. The FATF Recommendations 2012. p. 22. See also the requirement applicable to bearer shares under Element A.1.2 of the EOIR standard, as provided by the Global Forum. 2016. *Exchange of Information on Request: Handbook for Peer Reviews 2016–2020—2016 Terms of Reference.* Paris: OECD. p.19; It states that "where jurisdictions permit the issuance of bearer shares, they should have appropriate mechanisms in place that allow the owners of such shares to be identified. One possibility among others is a custodial arrangement with a recognised custodian or other similar arrangement to immobilise such shares."

On nominee shareholders and nominee directors, the revised FATF Recommendation 24 requires "countries that allow nominee shareholders or nominee directors to take effective measures to ensure that they are not misused for ML/TF [money laundering/terrorist financing] purposes" (footnote 11). The use of nominee shareholders or directors in the ownership and control structure of a legal entity hampers BOT efforts, as the natural person(s) whose name appears as a shareholder or owner or director in the shareholder register of a legal person is not the beneficial owner of the company—the beneficial owner's identity remains masked.

As discussed by E. F. Alpe during the joint ADB–EITI beneficial ownership workshop, the use of nominee shareholders becomes more complex in the case of listed companies, where, for instance, nominee companies are established by wealth managers to collectively hold all the shares in the listed company on behalf of their clients (footnote 99). In such instances, a wealth manager becomes the financial intermediary who acts as a proxy for the beneficiaries of nominee companies, who are typically high net worth individuals and family offices and are not named in the public share register (footnote 99).

Jurisdictions have adopted different approaches to deal with the risks associated with nominee shareholders and nominee directors. In some jurisdictions, nominees must expressly identify themselves to the legal entity, or the registration authority, or both.[112] As a good practice, such a disclosure should also be recorded in the register for cross-checking and verifying the accuracy of the beneficial ownership information disclosed in the centralized beneficial ownership register. Such required self-identification, including the stated sanctions specified for nominees who fail to properly disclose their status, is intended to increase transparency in the process of identifying beneficial owners. A few jurisdictions (such as the UK) also clearly provide in their legal and regulatory framework that claiming to be a nominee director does not exclude the nominee's personal criminal liability, and also restricts any indemnities in favor of nominees. There are some jurisdictions that completely prohibit nominee shareholders or nominee directors, while some require nominees to obtain licenses and reveal who they are acting for, with the information duly recorded and made available to a competent authority upon request.[113]

Important Considerations
• Enact proper provisions in the relevant laws and/or regulations to prohibit the issuance of new bearer shares or bearer share warrants, and to prevent the misuse of existing bearer shares or bearer share warrants.
• Take adequate measures to mitigate the risks associated with nominee shareholders and nominee directors, including obliging them to self-identify as a nominee to the relevant legal entity, as well as to the company registrar, so that the information can be properly recorded in the relevant registers.

---

[112]   For example, Nigeria and India for both nominee shareholders and nominee directors, Latvia for nominee directors, Australia for nominee directors, and Canada for nominee shareholders.

[113]   For example, nominee shareholders are prohibited in Spain, Brazil, Ukraine, Türkiye, Switzerland, and Argentina. Nominee directors are prohibited in Germany, Spain, the United States, Ukraine, Türkiye, Latvia, Switzerland, Canada, and Argentina. Licenses are required by Latvia and Canada for nominee shareholders and Australia for nominee directors.

B. Data Collection and Disclosure

Policy Considerations

As discussed in Section III-A of this study, the revised FATF Recommendations 2012 requires countries to adopt a multipronged approach to ensure that adequate, accurate, and up-to-date information on beneficial ownership is made available to the competent authorities rapidly and effectively. The FATF provides for three main approaches to obtain and hold the beneficial ownership information:

  a. the company approach,
  b. the beneficial ownership registry approach or alternate mechanisms, and
  c. the existing information approach.

During the joint ADB–EITI beneficial ownership workshop, Hakim Hamadi from the Global Forum highlighted some issues related to each of these approaches that should be taken into consideration by countries at the policy level (Table 5). In line with the FATF Recommendations, H. Hamadi recommended that countries adopt a multipronged approach for an effective BOT regime, to ensure that adequate, accurate, and up-to-date information on beneficial ownership is available to the competent authorities in a country.

Table 5: Beneficial Ownership Transparency Approaches: Issues to Be Considered by Countries

Company Approach	Beneficial Ownership Registry Approach	Existing Information or AML/CFT Approach
Insufficient coverage of entities	Insufficient coverage of entities	Insufficient coverage of entities
• Large number of unsupervised inactive entities. • Absence of registration with authorities or administrators of legal arrangements, particularly of foreign trusts.	• Large number of unsupervised inactive entities. • Absence of registration with authorities or administrators of legal arrangements, particularly of foreign trusts.	• Domestic legal persons and arrangements are not obliged to have a continuous relationship with an AML/CFT-obliged person, such as a DNFBP or a financial institution (e.g., bank account, accountant). • Relationship with the AML/CFT-obliged person is not continuous (e.g., notary).

continued on next page

Table 5 *(continued)*

Company Approach	Beneficial Ownership Registry Approach	Existing Information or AML/CFT Approach
Legal entities fail to accurately identify their beneficial owners and collect information on them	**Legal entities fail to accurately identify their beneficial owners and collect information on them**	**No regular updating of information or record-keeping**
• Beneficial ownership can be a new requirement for most legal persons and arrangements, with insufficient experience in beneficial ownership identification in line with the standard, particularly in the case of complex chains of ownership. • Deficiencies in the obligation to identify, verify, update, and keep records. • Insufficient training and guidance.	• Beneficial ownership can be a new requirement for most legal persons and arrangements, with insufficient experience in beneficial ownership identification in line with the standard, particularly in the case of complex chains of ownership. • Insufficient training and guidance.	• Different approaches are adopted for updating information (e.g., it depends on the risk of the client, without minimum requirements for low-risk clients). • Simplified CDD allows for easing the requirement regarding the identification of beneficial owners. • Record-keeping is not ensured when the AML/CFT person ceases their activity.
Inadequate supervisory authority	**Reliance on supervision by authorities without adequate mandates**	**Insufficient coverage of supervision, particularly in the case of DNFBPs.**
• Authorities without adequate powers, knowledge, experience, and/or resources to regularly supervise and enforce compliance among universe of entities, including administrators of legal arrangements and inactive entities.	• The central register is not supervised by an authority with the legal and institutional capacity to monitor and enforce obligations. • Reliance on supervision by existing registrars without strong monitoring functions, powers, and resources (e.g., commercial registrar).	
Difficulties in authorities gaining access to information	**Accessing information by authorities (public registers)**	**Difficulties in authorities gaining access to information**
• Identifying the holder of beneficial ownership information can be difficult; for example, when the administrator of a legal arrangement is not registered with a public authority, or a legal entity has ceased to exist.	• Access to tax authorities and other relevant competent authorities should be ensured. • Reporting of discrepancies in the beneficial ownership register should be ensured. • Depending on the scope, extent, criteria, and modalities defined for accessing beneficial ownership information maintained by the registrar, compliance with data protection and privacy issues should be ensured, particularly in the context of public central registers.	• Broad professional secrecy and privilege. • Difficulty in identifying the holder of beneficial ownership information.

AML/CFT = anti-money laundering/combating financing of terrorism, CDD = customer due diligence, DNFBP = designated nonfinancial businesses and professions.
Source: Hamadi, H. 2022. *Policy Approaches for Beneficial Ownership Implementation*. Presentation made during ADB and EITI Regional Workshop on Advancing Beneficial Ownership Transparency. 21–23 February.

The earlier FATF Recommendation 24 did not define the set of information on beneficial owners that should be collected, maintained, and disclosed under any of the above three approaches. Nonetheless, the recently revised FATF Recommendation 24 provides examples of information that should be collected by various stakeholders (including companies and reporting entities, as well as the register) to identify the natural person(s) who are beneficial owner(s). This information includes "the full name, nationality(ies), the full date and place of birth, residential address, national identification number and document type, and the tax identification number or equivalent in the country of residence."[114] The revised FATF Recommendation 24 also requires, under "adequate" beneficial ownership information, the identification of the means and mechanisms through which the beneficial owner exercises beneficial ownership or control. This is the minimum information on beneficial ownership, which, according to the revised FATF Recommendation 24, should be collected by legal entities under the company approach, by the designated authority under the beneficial ownership registry approach, and by the reporting entities under the existing information approach.

Similar to the revised FATF Recommendation 24, the EITI standard also sets out the key information that should be collected on beneficial owners for effective disclosure. This includes the name of the beneficial owner, the nature and percentage of ownership, PEP status, nationality, and the country of residence. The EITI standard also recommends that other information be disclosed, such as passport or citizenship number, date of birth, residential and service address, and means of contact (footnote 17).

In line with the above international standards, this study recommends that the relevant laws and/or regulations of jurisdictions should explicitly specify the minimum beneficial ownership information that should be obtained, maintained, and updated by legal entities, and submitted on the beneficial ownership register, if established. Specifying the minimum beneficial ownership information in the relevant laws and/or regulations will help ensure the collection of consistent and adequate minimum data on beneficial owners. From the analysis of legal and regulatory frameworks in some jurisdictions, it appears to be a good practice to collect the following minimum data on beneficial owners:

- official name of the beneficial owner (as it appears in the national identity card or passport)
- issue date and number of the national identity card or passport for domestic natural persons
- passport number, issue date, and issuing state for foreign natural persons
- date and place of birth
- nationality or citizenship
- country of residence
- residential address
- correspondence or service address, if it differs from the residential address
- tax identification number

---

[114]   The FATF Recommendations 2012. INR 24. p. 94.

- form in which beneficial ownership is held—ownership share (the exact percentage of shares or percentage of share in capital, or the exact percentage of voting rights, or data on the percentage of indirect or direct share in the property/assets of the legal person or other foreign legal entity) or other type of control (a determining influence in controlling the legal persons, whether the natural persons indirectly provide or have provided funds, or have a determining influence on decision-making or control management)
- date when the natural persons acquired such control
- the date of any change in beneficial ownership information—becoming or ceasing to be the beneficial owner of a legal person
- details of the authorized person or DNFBP responsible for submitting the beneficial ownership information on behalf of the legal entity
- identification of PEPs, including their family members and known close associates.

Another policy consideration for data collection, especially in the case of the registry approach, is whether to add the beneficial ownership information to an existing system or to create a stand-alone system. This depends largely on the level of sophistication of the company register already in place, and the available resources. Some jurisdictions, such as the UK, collect and add the beneficial ownership information or data to an existing company register, whereas others, such as Austria and Slovakia, have created a completely separate beneficial ownership register for collecting and maintaining the beneficial ownership data.

The countries also need to ensure that the data contained in the register is kept up-to-date and that the designated authority or agency has the necessary legal mandate, means, and resources to confirm and verify the currency of beneficial ownership data. In this regard, relevant laws or regulations should provide for a clearly specified time frame for the companies to update their beneficial ownership information in the register after the occurrence of any changes in their beneficial owner(s). In the UK and Ireland, for instance, companies are required to update their internal beneficial ownership records within 14 days of any change in beneficial ownership, and to convey such changes to the central beneficial ownership register within a further 14 days (i.e., a total of 28 days).

Similarly, Belgium gives a period of 1 month to send any changes in the data of beneficial ownership to its central register. However, some jurisdictions give a much shorter time frame for legal persons to update their beneficial ownership information in the register. These include, for instance, Indonesia (3 working days), the Philippines (7 days), Montenegro (8 days), North Macedonia (8 days), Serbia (15 days), and Malaysia (14 days to report beneficial ownership changes to the registrar [a beneficial ownership register has not yet been established in Malaysia]).

The recently revised FATF Recommendation 24 states that the beneficial ownership information should be updated within a "reasonable period" following any changes. It does not elaborate on the term "reasonable period" but gives the example of "within one month." This study recommends countries to determine this "reasonable period" for updating the beneficial ownership information based on the findings of their national risk assessment regarding legal persons and legal arrangements within their jurisdiction. However, it is strongly recommended that the period should not be more than 30 days after the occurrence of any changes in the beneficial owner(s).

To ensure the accuracy of available data on beneficial ownership, a few countries, such as Austria, Belgium, Denmark, Ukraine, and the UK, also require legal entities to confirm the accuracy of the current information on an annual basis.[115] In the UK, for instance, legal entities are required to confirm their beneficial ownership data with Companies House each year via the confirmation statement—the statement which they are required to submit no later than 14 days from the end of the last 12-month period. Regarding any updates on beneficial ownership information submitted to the internal revenue or tax department of the jurisdiction, they could form a part of the annual return submitted to the department.

Technical and Practical Considerations

Under the company approach and the existing information approach, as highlighted during the joint ADB–EITI workshop, it is important for both legal entities and the reporting entities under the AML/CFT law to understand the entire ownership and control structure of an entity and to collect the relevant documents. This includes, for instance, extracts from the company register to understand shareholdings at each level of the structure, any shareholder agreements, articles of association, statement of capital, and powers of attorney, including any trust or foundation deeds and letters of wishes, if trusts or foundations feature in the ownership or control structure. Companies and reporting entities could collect these documents either in electronic or paper form, but it is important to ensure the accuracy and reliability of these documents (this is discussed in more detail in the next section).

For the registry approach, an important technical consideration for authorities in collecting beneficial ownership data is how this data should be collected and stored. The data collection mechanisms vary across countries. The beneficial ownership data can be collected using a variety of tools, including questionnaires and templates in PDF and Excel, fully integrated web portals, and bespoke databases.[116] However, it is crucial to remember that the scale of the solution should correspond to the extent of the data being gathered, and should facilitate data availability to the public.

The countries researched for the purposes of this study have reported many technical barriers and challenges with respect to data collection and verification. These include the collection of beneficial ownership data in paper format (e.g., Kyrgyz Republic EITI beneficial ownership declarations), in spreadsheet form (e.g., Kazakhstan mining license data), or through emails (e.g., as scanned PDFs in the Philippines); the lack of technical and human resources to process the applications; and the conversion of the submitted data into a structured format that can be made available to the public

---

[115] Knobel, A. 2019. Beneficial Ownership Verification: Ensuring the Truthfulness and Accuracy of Registered Ownership Information. *Tax Justice Network*. 22 January. p. 33.

[116] For bespoke databases, see Open Extractives. 2021. *Relational Database Design Considerations for Beneficial Ownership Information*. Technical Guidance. 16 December. https://openownershiporgprod-1b54.kxcdn.com/media/documents/oo-guidance-relational-database-design-technical-guidance-english-2021-12.pdf (accessed 6 June 2021).

or can be easily linked to other datasets. It is therefore important for authorities to ensure, at a technical level, that the required beneficial ownership data is collected in a structured format so that it can be easily linked to other datasets and made available to the public.

As highlighted by Louise Russell-Prywata during the joint ADB–EITI beneficial ownership workshop, compared to unstructured data, which is likely to require data science expertise or much time to search, compare, and link declarations, structured data makes it easy to search, compare, and link various declarations.[117] Digitalized submission would also improve the data quality. Open Ownership's Beneficial Ownership Data Standard (BODS), for instance, has been endorsed by organizations, such as EITI and the Open Contracting Partnership, for collecting high-quality data electronically. Countries such as Armenia, Latvia, Ukraine, and Nigeria have been implementing the BODS, in collaboration with Open Ownership, to collect relevant beneficial ownership data (footnote 51). In essence, the BODS offers a standardized data format together with guidance for collecting, sharing, and utilizing high-quality beneficial ownership data. It is structured around the concept of statements which describe a person, entities (including companies, trusts, and arrangements), and ownership or control of entities by a person (Table 6). These statements, when combined, can explain and visualize simple or complex beneficial ownership structures.

Table 6: Fields within Different Types of Statements in the Beneficial Ownership Data Standard

Person	Entity	Ownership or Control
• Statement ID, type, and date • Person type • Unspecified person details • Names • Identifiers • Nationalities • Place of birth • Birth date • Place of residence • Tax residencies • Addresses • Has PEP status • Provenance (source/annotations/ replaces statement)	• Statement ID, type, and date • Entity type • Unspecified entity details • Name • Alternate names • Jurisdiction • Identifiers • Founding date • Dissolution date • Addresses • Provenance (source/annotations/ replaces statement)	• Statement ID, type, and date • Component • Component statement IDs • Subject • Interested party • Interests • Provenance (source/annotations/ replaces statement)

ID = identification, PEP = politically exposed person.
Source: Russell-Prywata, L. 2022. *BO Data Collection and Disclosure: Technical and Practical Considerations*. Presentation made during ADB and EITI Regional Workshop on Advancing Beneficial Ownership Transparency. 21– 23 February.

---

[117]   Russell-Prywata, L. 2022. *BO Data Collection and Disclosure: Technical and Practical Considerations*. Presentation made during ADB and EITI Regional Workshop on Advancing Beneficial Ownership Transparency. 21–23 February.

For agencies tasked with implementing the beneficial ownership requirement of the EITI standard, the EITI has also developed two beneficial ownership model declaration forms for basic and high-quality data collection (the latter is compatible with BODS) to support the implementation of Requirement 2.5 of the EITI standard.[118] The basic data collection form is most suitable for countries with a small number of companies and lower technical capacity to collect and publish data. The high-quality data collection form is in Excel format and is most useful as a basis for countries designing an online form and in helping ensure that the collected beneficial ownership data can be linked with existing government data or made publicly available through an online register.

At a technical level, relevant authorities also need to ensure not only that the beneficial ownership data is stored in a structured format but also that the database makes it possible to store historical data on beneficial owners, which should be non-destructive (i.e., the system allows the data to be replaced rather than updated). There should be a proper legal basis for the treatment of historical data in relevant laws and regulations, which must conform with the domestic and international data protection laws and allow for the removal or alteration of inaccurate information or information that is likely to cause harm.

When discussing challenges related to beneficial ownership data collection, another significant challenge that came to light during discussions with speakers and participants at the joint ADB–EITI beneficial ownership workshop is the lack of awareness among companies about the concept of beneficial ownership, its significance, their beneficial ownership disclosure obligations, and the information they must disclose relating to beneficial owners.

In Indonesia, for instance, since the establishment of the central beneficial ownership register in December 2020, only 24.50% of corporations had disclosed their beneficial ownership information to the register up to 28 November 2021 (footnote 57). The lack of education and awareness among corporations in Indonesia about the significance of BOT and their beneficial ownership disclosure obligations has been highlighted as one of the major causes of this low level of reporting (footnote 57). The joint ADB–EITI beneficial ownership workshop clearly highlighted the significance of awareness-raising and outreach activities involving legal entities, in regard to the concept of beneficial ownership and disclosure requirements. L. Russell-Prywata also highlighted the significance of designing good digital beneficial ownership data collection forms to ensure that high-quality data is collected (footnote 117).

---

[118]   These beneficial ownership model declaration forms are available at EITI. Guidance: Beneficial Ownership Model Declaration Form. https://eiti.org/documents/beneficial-ownership-model-declaration-form (accessed 6 June 2022).

Important Considerations

- Require legal persons to keep an in-house beneficial ownership register containing certain minimum beneficial ownership data, and to make the register available to the public.
- Specify certain requirements regarding the minimum beneficial ownership information that should be obtained, maintained, and updated by the reporting entities, and by the legal persons, in the beneficial ownership register.
- In laws and/or regulations, specify a clear time frame for legal persons to report and update the beneficial ownership information in the central register.
- Incorporate a provision in the law that requires the relevant designated authority to maintain the beneficial ownership information for a minimum 5-year period after the dissolution of the company, which might be extended to an additional 5 years in certain circumstances (e.g., detection or investigation of a criminal offense), in conformity with data protection and privacy laws.
- Ensure that corporate vehicles are aware of the concept of beneficial ownership, its significance, and their beneficial ownership-related requirements by conducting sufficient awareness-raising and outreach activities.

C. Data Verification

Verification of the beneficial ownership information, whether by legal entities under the company approach, reporting entities under the existing information approach, or registries under the registry approach, has been identified as a major challenge by countries worldwide, as well as by Asia and Pacific countries selected for this study. This is largely because of the intricate structures and layers of ownership, which span many jurisdictions and include various kinds of legal persons and/or legal arrangements, which makes it complex and challenging for various stakeholders to adequately identify and verify the information on beneficial owners (footnote 99). Further complexity in the entire beneficial ownership verification process arises because even corporate entities (as extensively discussed during the joint ADB–EITI workshop) are unfamiliar with the concept of beneficial ownership, especially in the case of smaller companies, on which the onus has been placed in most jurisdictions to obtain, maintain, and report beneficial ownership information, and to provide the supporting documentation where required.

During the joint ADB–EITI workshop, E. F. Alpe emphasized the significance of identification and verification of beneficial ownership information and the role of civil society, competent authorities, financial institutions, and DNFBPs in the verification process (footnote 99). To verify the beneficial ownership information of legal entities, financial institutions and DNFBPs could ask for documents such as the shareholder register, which should be certified by the senior management of the company, a company secretary, or a professional (for example, a practicing lawyer, an accountant, or a notary); articles of association; shareholder agreements; minutes of any previous board or shareholder meetings; powers of attorney; lists of members of board of directors; and lists of all senior managing officials. For foundations or trusts, the documents for verification could be a trust or foundation deed, a letter of wishes, or a power of attorney. During the workshop, the lack of uniform rules on beneficial ownership disclosure across jurisdictions and the lack of publicly available information on beneficial ownership were highlighted as major obstacles in the beneficial ownership data verification process (footnote 99). The significance of having a digital online beneficial ownership platform as one of the mechanisms for identifying and verifying beneficial ownership information was also emphasized.

Clearly, effective verification is essential for BOT in a particular jurisdiction, as well as for the beneficial ownership register to be a reliable tool for enhancing transparency and combating financial crime. A key challenge for any beneficial ownership register, as also highlighted by Stephen Abbott Pugh during the joint ADB–EITI beneficial ownership workshop, is to ensure the completeness and accuracy of the initial data collected, and its integrity over time by ensuring that data is periodically updated. This is also an issue identified under the company approach and the existing information approach. With respect to the registry approach, while highlighting the Open Ownership Principles, S. A. Pugh discussed that this could be achieved through a robust verification system, involving a combination of checks and processes, which can be introduced in three different steps to ensure the quality, trustworthiness, and reliability of beneficial ownership data:

- Step 1: Pre-submission—when the beneficial ownership disclosure is submitted, in the form of information about the person, an entity, and the control relationship between them.
- Step 2: At the point of submission of beneficial ownership information—when a number of verification checks (including conformance, cross-checks, and supporting documentation checks) can be performed.
- Step 3: After the submission of beneficial ownership information—when any errors, omissions, and discrepancies are reported (for instance, by competent authorities, reporting entities, non-profit organizations, or the public) and the data requires correction or resubmission.[119]

The Open Ownership diagram in Figure 4 depicts the verification workflow.

---

[119] Open Ownership. 2020. *Verification of Beneficial Ownership Data.* Policy Briefing. May. https://openownershiporgprod-1b54.kxcdn.com/media/documents/oo-briefing-verification-briefing-2020-05.pdf.

Figure 4: Open Ownership's Beneficial Ownership Data Verification Steps

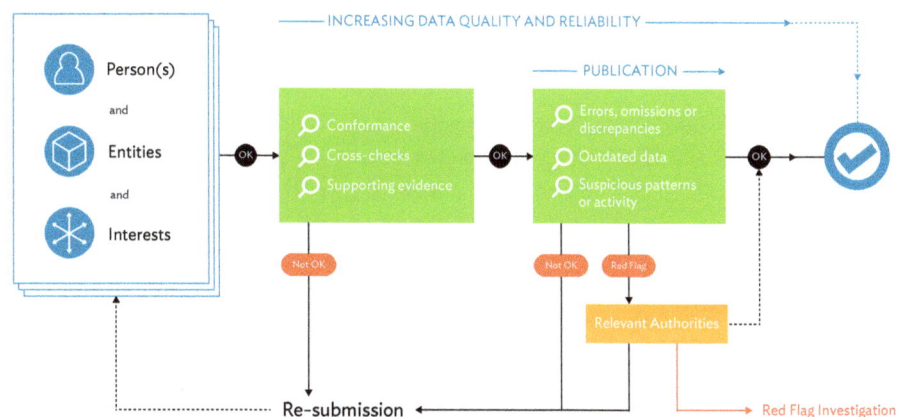

Source: Open Ownership. 2020. Verification of Beneficial Ownership Data. Policy Briefing. May. p. 3.

This section discusses some of the common challenges faced by countries in the verification process, highlights the best practices, and offers recommendations for addressing these challenges.

Step 1 and Step 2: Pre-Submission and Submission

Ensuring the accuracy of the beneficial ownership information submitted and available is one of the major challenges that countries face. Mistaken or fraudulent submissions remain a key challenge for beneficial ownership databases in most countries, including the UK.[120] Because of various resource constraints (both technical and human), the information submitted is often not actively verified, tested, or monitored by the designated authorities. In most jurisdictions, no authority has in fact been designated or given the responsibility to verify the beneficial ownership data submitted. A lack of sufficient capacity on the part of the relevant authorities has often been reported as one of the major hindrances to ensuring the accuracy and adequacy of the beneficial ownership information on the register (footnote 56).

At the point of submission, some of the verification challenges faced by jurisdictions include the following:

- Corporate entities are unaware of, or unfamiliar with, the concept of beneficial ownership upon whom the obligation is placed in most jurisdictions to obtain, maintain, and report beneficial ownership information and to provide the supporting documentation, where required.

---

[120] In the UK, the initial analysis of the beneficial ownership information submitted to its beneficial ownership register has found a lot of discrepancies and breaches of law. For details, see Open Ownership. 2017. *Learning the Lessons from the UK's Public Beneficial Ownership Register*. October.

- It is difficult to verify beneficial ownership information given the complex corporate structures, particularly when there are multiple layers of ownership, involving multiple countries and a variety of legal entities and/or legal arrangements (such as trusts, foundations, joint stock companies, and public limited companies).
- Accidental errors or deliberate falsehoods occur when the beneficial ownership reporting system or mechanisms have not been properly designed (e.g., conformance of data and cross-checks) or when no authority has been designated to check and verify the submitted beneficial ownership information.

Despite these challenges, it is important to ensure that the beneficial ownership register does not play a passive role, simply acting as a repository of information or documents, and that there are proper mechanisms in place to verify and monitor the quality and accuracy of the information received and held in the register.

To ensure that beneficial ownership information is adequate, accurate, and updated in a timely manner, various international standards require legal entities to authorize one or more natural persons who are resident in the country or a DNFBP to provide the required beneficial ownership information to the register.[121] In compliance with these standards, many jurisdictions require that there is an authorized person who is a resident in the jurisdiction and who is responsible for disclosing the necessary beneficial ownership information to the register. Such an authorized declaring person can be a beneficial owner himself or herself, but in many instances, they may be a company advisor (such as a lawyer, auditor, or consultant) or a notary, who is also required in some countries to certify the accuracy of the beneficial ownership information submitted to the register (Boxes 1 and 2).

Box 1: Beneficial Ownership Declaration—The Case of Slovakia

In Slovakia, the beneficial ownership information contained in the Register of Public Sector Partners must be filed by an authorized person, who may be a lawyer, a notary, an auditor, or a tax advisor. Under Section 5(6) of the Law on the Register of Public Sector Partners, it is the obligation of an authorized person to provide true and complete information in the application for the registration of beneficial ownership data in the register. The law also obliges an authorized person to notify the registrar within 60 days from the date on which any changes in the beneficial ownership data occur, and to update the beneficial ownership information and the verification document (Section 9).

Source: Law on the Register of Public Sector Partners 2016, Slovakia.

---

[121]   See FATF. 2014. *Guidance on Transparency and Beneficial Ownership*. Paris. October. p. 27; footnote 57 where it states that "[b]oard members of senior management may not require specific authorisation by the company, as this might already fall within the scope of their authority;" and FATF Recommendations 2012. INR 24. p. 93.

Box 2: Beneficial Ownership Declaration—The Case of Denmark

In Denmark, Danish natural and legal persons are required to use a unique form of identification (NemID), granted by a government body, when they establish or manage legal entities, by submitting information for registration in the Danish Central Business Register (CVR). NemID is a widely used, secure internet login that may be used for a number of things, including online banking, getting information from government authorities, and interacting with businesses. The Danish Business Authority receives digital information on the person registering through this electronic login that can be utilized for verification purposes, leaving an electronic footprint in the process.

Further, when making a registration in the CVR, the declaring person signs an electronic declaration stating that the information entered into the business register is correct.

Source: FATF and Egmont Group. 2018. *Concealment of Beneficial Ownership*. Paris. p. 67. https://www.fatf-gafi.org/media/fatf/documents/reports/FATF-Egmont-Concealment-beneficial-ownership.pdf. https://www.fatf-gafi.org/media/fatf/documents/reports/FATF-Egmont-Concealment-beneficial-ownership.pdf.

The EITI standard also suggests that "companies attest to the beneficial ownership declaration form through a sign-off by a member of the senior management team or senior legal counsel, or by submitting supporting documentation" (footnote 17). Some jurisdictions have incorporated these mechanisms, at least in their legislative and regulatory framework, to verify the authenticity of the beneficial ownership information, but it is difficult to assess their effectiveness in practice. Only a very few existing operational beneficial ownership regimes (e.g., Belgium and Austria) have put in place data verification processes, including the submission of supporting documentation online.

Some of the measures taken by countries in their legislative and regulatory frameworks that emerge as best practices for verifying the data at the beneficial ownership submission stage include the following:

- Requiring legal entities to authorize and declare at least one natural person who is resident in the country to be accountable to the competent authorities for providing all the basic information and available beneficial ownership information, and for giving further assistance to the authorities.[122]
- Requiring legal entities to authorize and declare a DNFBP in the country who will be accountable to the competent authorities for providing beneficial ownership information to the registry and any other assistance (footnote 122)
- Imposing an obligation on beneficial owners to declare themselves and provide the necessary information to the concerned legal person so that such information can be registered in the beneficial ownership register.[123]

---

[122]   FATF Recommendations 2012. INR 24. para 9.
[123]   See, for instance, Article 30 (1) (ii), EU 5th AML Directive. Measure Incorporated in the BO Regime of the United Kingdom.

- Imposing an obligation on beneficial owners under the law or regulations requiring them to certify the accuracy and completeness of the beneficial ownership information in the register.
- Requiring the submission of scanned copies of relevant documents, such as a national identity card or passport, a copy of the share register, or a shareholders' agreement, to the online registry.[124]
- Providing sufficient and effective sanctions and enforcement powers to the designated authority, as well as incorporating dissuasive, proportionate, and effective sanctions for any breaches of beneficial ownership disclosure requirements.

At the technical level, to ensure the adequacy and authenticity of the beneficial ownership data at the point of submission, a number of solutions have emerged in recent years, which perform conformance checks on the beneficial ownership data and cross-check it with other databases held nationally and internationally. A few countries (e.g., Armenia, Belgium, Latvia, and Denmark) have developed and built their beneficial ownership data registration systems in such a manner that they can identify and highlight any discrepancies in the beneficial ownership data at the point of submission (Boxes 3 and 4). Business rules have been embedded in the beneficial ownership registration platform and applied during the registration process to avoid registering incoherent or erroneous information (e.g., shares or voting rights exceeding 100%, registering dead or unborn beneficial owners, or pre-registration of already known and "certified" information).[125]

Box 3: Conformance Checks in Belgium

In the Belgian Ultimate Beneficial Owners (UBO) Register, the system prevents the registration of more than 100% of the shares/voting rights for an individual, as well as the registration of a deceased person or a Belgian national that is not registered in the national register of natural persons, as this would not technically be possible, thereby ensuring that data conforms to expected patterns.

Source: FATF. 2019. *Best Practices on Beneficial Ownership for Legal Persons*. Paris. p. 47. https://www.fatf-gafi.org/media/fatf/documents/Best-Practices-Beneficial-Ownership-Legal-Persons.pdf.

---

[124] See Open Ownership. 2017. *Learning the Lessons from the UK's Public Beneficial Ownership Register*. October. p. 9; and Bruun, B. 2017. *Mandatory Registration of Beneficial Owners*. Lexology. 31 May; In Belgium, since 11 October 2020, it has been made mandatory to submit pertinent supporting documents (e.g., copy of the share register; articles of association; shareholders' agreement; a notarial deed or any other document which is to be legalized/notarized if originating from a third country) to the beneficial ownership register to ensure that the information is adequate, accurate, and current.

[125] In the United Kingdom, not setting the proper business validation rules at the launch of the beneficial ownership register has had a huge impact on the quality and accuracy of the resulting data. For details, see Open Ownership. 2017. *Learning the Lessons from the UK's Public Beneficial Ownership Register*. October.

> ### Box 4: Cross-Checks in Denmark
>
> The Danish Central Business Register (CVR) automatically cross-checks the information given with a number of official records, such as the civil register and the Danish address registry. The system prevents, for example, the registration of a deceased person.
>
> Source: Open Ownership. 2020. Verification of Beneficial Ownership Data. Policy Briefing (May). p. 5. https://openownershiporgprod-1b54.kxcdn.com/media/documents/oo-briefing-verification-briefing-2020-05.pdf.

Step 3: After the Submission of Beneficial Ownership Information

Verification is a constant process and countries should ensure that the data submitted to the beneficial ownership register is verified not only at the point of submission but also after submission, to ensure that it is accurate and up-to-date. Continuous verification of the beneficial ownership data has often been reported by countries as another major challenge since the beneficial ownership information is likely to change continuously over time.

In this regard, several measures have been investigated and implemented by countries seeking to develop negative or positive incentives for complying with the beneficial ownership requirements, assigning responsibilities, targeting controls, and avoiding good faith mistakes. The following measures (among others) have emerged as best practices for ensuring the adequacy and accuracy of beneficial ownership data:

- The role of reporting entities and competent authorities under the AML/CFT law of a country. Imposing an obligation on reporting entities (as defined under the AML/CFT law) and competent authorities to notify the designated authority on any discrepancies between the information they have and the information registered in the beneficial ownership register has been identified as an important mechanism for ensuring the accuracy of the beneficial ownership data recorded in the register.[126] The revised FATF Recommendation 24 also recommends that such a measure (i.e., discrepancy reporting) be considered by countries as a complementary measure to support the accuracy of beneficial ownership information.[127]
- Sample checking by the designated authority. Authorizing the designated authority in charge of the beneficial ownership register (e.g., in Denmark) to use its own internal or external resources to conduct sample checks and/or analysis and cross-checking of the submitted data can serve as an important mechanism for enhancing the quality of beneficial ownership data. As this can be very resource-intensive, adopting a risk-based approach when selecting the sample of legal entities for beneficial ownership verification checks can be useful.

---

[126] See, for instance, EU 5th AML Directive. Article 30 (4). Measure Incorporated in the Beneficial Ownership Regime of UK and Majority EU Member States.

[127] FATF Recommendations 2012. INR 24. p. 94.

- Qualitative controls. This measure, which is much more complex and time-consuming than the two others, involves the use of data mining tools in analyzing the registered data based on established and observed behavioral patterns or characteristics.[128] This kind of data analysis has proven to be very effective in other areas of enforcement (e.g., tax fraud). However, it implies the need to train data miners and analysts, and to invest in specialized software. These data mining controls and procedures can be considered as "mature" after a period of about 6 years. They are therefore a long-term investment. Making sure that such analytical tools can be applied to the beneficial ownership register at a later stage is important to the architecture and structure of the database.
- The role of civil society and the public. Civil society and the public can play a significant role in verifying the adequacy and accuracy of the beneficial ownership data submitted to the register, provided that the beneficial ownership data is available publicly (Box 5). A study conducted by the Open Ownership suggests that the "publication of beneficial ownership data publicly can drive up data quality, as increased data use drives up the likelihood of inconsistencies or potential wrongdoings being identified."[129]

Box 5: Public Access—The Case of the United Kingdom

In November 2016, Global Witness and a consortium of nongovernment organizations analyzed 1.3 million companies in the central beneficial ownership register of the United Kingdom (UK). They were able to inform Companies House in the UK, the body overseeing the register, that more than 4,000 companies had ineligible information.

Sources: Open Ownership. 2020. Verification of Beneficial Ownership Data. Policy Briefing (May). p. 7. https://openownershipprod-1b54.kxcdn.com/media/documents/oo-briefing-verification-briefing-2020-05.pdf; Global Witness. 2018. The Companies We Keep: What the UK's Open Data Register Actually Tells Us about Company Ownership. July. https://www.globalwitness.org/en/campaigns/corruption-and-money-laundering/anonymous-company-owners/companies-we-keep/.

Countries need to discuss and explore the various beneficial ownership data verification mechanisms that might work best for their respective situations.

---

128 See Open Ownership. 2022. *Our Initial Assessment of Myanmar's New Beneficial Ownership Register.* March. https://www.openownership.org/news/our-initial-assessment-of-myanmars-new-beneficial-ownership-register/.

129 Footnote 119, p. 7. See also Open Ownership. 2020. *Briefing: The Case for Beneficial Ownership as Open Data.* Policy Briefing (July 2017). https://www.openownership.org/uploads/briefing-on-beneficial-ownership-as-open-data.pdf.

<table>
<tr><td>Important Considerations</td></tr>
</table>

- Provide clear guidelines to legal entities and reporting entities on the beneficial ownership data to be obtained and maintained under the entire ownership and control structure of a legal entity.
- Establish, both at the policy and technical levels, effective verification and validation measures at all three stages of the verification process: pre-submission, submission, and after submission of the beneficial ownership data.
- Apply a combination of different verification mechanisms at various steps to ensure their effectiveness.

D. Registration and Public Disclosure

The advantages of public access to beneficial ownership information cannot be overstated. Public access not only improves the overall transparency of the business environment, but it is also a crucial component of beneficial ownership data verification. It allows scrutiny by a variety of interested stakeholders, as well as reporting of any unusual details or information that seems missing or inaccurate. In the Philippines, for instance, the role played by civil society in highlighting some of the inconsistencies in the reported beneficial ownership data to the SEC and the EITI was clearly highlighted by Vincent Lazatin during the joint ADB–EITI beneficial ownership workshop, including cases where the disclosure of ownership does not add up to 100% ownership.[130]

Nonetheless, the discussions on providing access to potentially sensitive information on the beneficial ownership register have proven to be contentious internationally. The FATF standards do not contain any requirement to make this information public. It simply requires countries to put in place mechanisms that ensure that the beneficial ownership information on legal persons is available and accessible to the competent authorities in a timely manner. A similar provision can also be found in UNCAC Article 12, which requires that state parties take measures to "safeguard the integrity of private entities, [...] by inter alia [...] establishing measures regarding the identity of legal and natural persons involved in the establishment and management of corporate entities."

However, the EITI standard and the EU Fifth AML Directive require their member countries to establish a beneficial ownership register (which is limited to the extractives sector in the case of the EITI standard) and to make this information freely accessible to the public.[131] The EU Fifth AML Directive requires, for instance, the following information on beneficial owners, at a minimum, to be accessible to the public—"the name, the month and year of birth, the country of residence and nationality of the beneficial owner, and the nature and extent of the beneficial interest held" (footnote 131). The EITI also has certain requirements regarding the minimum information on beneficial owners that should be made available to the public— name, nationality, country of residence of beneficial owner(s), as well as identifying any PEPs (footnote 131).

---

[130] Lazatin, V. 2022. *Beneficial Ownership Disclosures: A Civil Society Perspective.* Presentation made during ADB and EITI Regional Workshop on Advancing Beneficial Ownership Transparency. 21– 23 February.
[131] EITI Standard 2019. Requirement 2.5 (a); EU 5th AML Directive. Article 30 (5).

Although the FATF standards do not require the beneficial ownership information to be made public, international good practice appears to be moving in the direction of public access to beneficial ownership registers. To effectively combat the misuse of corporate entities for money laundering, terrorist financing, and corruption, it is now widely accepted that the best practice is to make beneficial ownership information accessible to the public. Many jurisdictions (such as the UK, Belgium, Ukraine, Denmark, Ireland, and Armenia) have established centralized and public beneficial ownership registries that are available and accessible to the public. Some jurisdictions, however, charge a small fee for accessing the beneficial ownership register, to recover costs (for example, Belgium and Ireland).

Even if a jurisdiction opts to charge a fee, it is considered a best practice for the fee to be a nominal one and it "[should] not exceed the administrative costs of making the information available, including costs of maintenance and development of the register."[132] This practice of charging a fee to access the beneficial ownership information varies from country to country. For instance, in the UK, access to the beneficial ownership register is available completely free of charge, even when it is estimated that the economic value of the beneficial ownership information contained in the register is roughly £400 million (per the information provided by representatives of the Department of Business, Energy and Industrial Strategy

[BEIS] and Companies House [UK] during their presentation at the joint ADB–EITI beneficial ownership workshop).[133] In Ireland, which established its beneficial ownership register in 2019, a nominal fee of €2.50 is charged to access the central register. Most jurisdictions tend to make the beneficial ownership information available free of charge, with the intention of promoting wider access to this information, which may in turn lead to ensuring the submission of high-quality data and enhance data accuracy by enabling data users (such as those from the private sector, civil society, and the public sector) to evaluate and report any errors in the data.[134]

Another data publication issue that has been identified in the jurisdictions selected for the purposes of this study relates to balancing and/or resolving any potential conflict between the beneficial ownership disclosures and data protection or privacy concerns.

---

[132] EU 5th AML Directive. Article 30(5a); For instance, in Indonesia, a fee of around $3 is charged to access the register and for each requested information, which might not be a small fee for the reporting entities and other stakeholders in the country. It will hinder the process of ensuring accountability and transparency which is the entire purpose of establishing a beneficial ownership register.

[133] Vail, N., and L. Robins. 2022. *UK's Register of Company Beneficial Owners: The People with Significant Control (PSC) Register.* Presentation made during ADB and EITI Regional Workshop on Advancing Beneficial Ownership Transparency. 21–23 February.

[134] In the United Kingdom, for instance, Companies House confirmed that within the first 6 months of launching their beneficial ownership register, they were contacted by multiple parties from the public, highlighting inaccuracies in the data. See Open Ownership. 2017. *Learning the Lessons from the UK's Public Beneficial Ownership Register.* October. p. 3.

To determine what information should be made available to the public, there should be two considerations: (i) the information's usefulness to the public, and (ii) any potential privacy or security issues for specific beneficial owners. A clear provision should be included in the relevant law or regulations to specify the information that will be made accessible to the public.

At the international level, as a best practice, the minimum information on beneficial ownership that is generally made accessible to the public includes the name, the month and year of birth, the nationality and country of residence, the correspondence and business address, the nature and extent of the beneficial interest held, and the period for which such an interest was held. However, in accordance with the domestic legislation and data protection laws and rules, a country may decide to disclose additional information (for example, the last four digits of national registration cards [NRC] or date of birth) to enable the identification of the beneficial owner. Table 7 shows an example of the type of beneficial ownership information that could be made available to the public—an approach taken by the UK.

Table 7: Summary of "Persons of Significant Control" Information Relating to an Individual Required and Made Available Under Normal Circumstance: An Example from the United Kingdom

Information the company must collect about its PSCs, hold on the company's own PSC register, and file at Companies House. This information will be available to law enforcement and credit reference agencies.	PSC information the company must provide in response to requests for copies of its own PSC register.	PSC information Companies House will make available on the central public register.	PSC information Companies House will make available on the central public register if the company chooses to keep its own register at Companies House.
Name	Name	Name	Name
Full date of birth	Full date of birth	Month and year of birth	Full date of birth
Nationality	Nationality	Nationality	Nationality
Country/area of residence	Country/area of residence	Country/area of residence	Country/area of residence
Service address	Service address	Service address	Service address
Residential address			
Date became a PSC	Date became a PSC	Date became a PSC	Date became a PSC
Which of the conditions for being a PSC are met	Which of the conditions for being a PSC are met	Which of the conditions for being a PSC are met	Which of the conditions for being a PSC are met

Note: In the United Kingdom, the term "Persons of Significant Control" (PSC) is used to refer to beneficial owners.
Source: Government of the United Kingdom, Department for Business, Energy and Industrial Strategy. 2017. Guidance for People with Significant Control over Companies, SOCIETATES EUROPAEAE, Limited Liability Partnerships and Eligible Scottish Partnerships. June.

When granting public access to the beneficial ownership information of legal persons, it is also important to include relevant legal provisions that enable the beneficial owners to apply for an exemption from granting public access to all or a part of their information if the disclosure of this information would expose the beneficial owner to a disproportionate risk, or a "risk of fraud, kidnapping, blackmail, extortion, harassment, violence, or intimidation, or where the beneficial owner is a minor or otherwise legally incapable."[135] Even when such an exemption to public disclosure is granted, it should be ensured (by incorporating a relevant provision in the legislation) that the full beneficial ownership information is available to the competent authorities (like in the case of the UK).

It is recommended that to understand such exemption, a provision should be incorporated in the relevant laws and/or regulations that requires the relevant designated authority to annually publish statistical data on the number of such exemption applications received, granted, rejected, or pending, as well as the reasons behind the decisions. Such provisions have been incorporated in the legislation in the UK—between April 2016 and December 2018, Companies House received 903 applications from beneficial owners to protect their details from public disclosure. Out of these applications, 214 applications were rejected or refused, 215 were awaiting a decision, 402 were granted protection of their residential address, and only 74 (16%) were granted full exemption or protection from public disclosure of their beneficial ownership information.[136]

This study also recommends that relevant laws and/or regulations provide further details on how this request for exemption should be submitted by authorized persons or beneficial owners (e.g., there may be a separate form to submit this information), the supporting evidence required to demonstrate the risk, the timescale for reporting the decision by the relevant authority, whether this decision can be appealed, and (if yes) if there is any limitation.[137] To ensure that applying for an exemption does not become a norm, the burden should be placed on the party that invokes the exemption to substantiate it. In the UK, for instance, the evidence required to support an application to grant exemption from public disclosure of beneficial ownership information includes (i) a police incident number if the applicant has been attacked; (ii) documentary evidence of a threat or attack, such as photos or recordings; (iii) evidence of possible disruption or targeting, such as by animal rights or other activists; and (iv) evidence that the applicant works for an organization whose activities put them at risk, such as the Secret Intelligence Service (footnote 137).

To decide on the application, Companies House has been given the power to request that an assessment be carried out by a relevant authority regarding the nature and level of risk.

---

[135]   EU 5th AML Directive. Article 30 (9).

[136]   Government of the United Kingdom, Department for Business, Energy and Industrial Strategy. 2019. *Post Implementation Review of the People of Significant Control Register.* October. pp. 23–24. https://www.legislation.gov.uk/uksi/2017/694/pdfs/uksiod_20170694_en.pdf.

[137]   For further details on the provisions incorporated in the UK legislation, see GOV.UK. Applying to Protect Your Personal Information on the Companies House Register. https://www.gov.uk/guidance/applying-to-protect-your-personal-information-on-the-companies-house-register (accessed 27 April 2022).

Overall, a country must take a policy decision about the level of access to be provided, ensuring that the beneficial ownership register is open to public, but there are measures in place to protect privacy and prevent security threats. The authorities have to decide on the details of the beneficial ownership data that will be disclosed to the public, whether access needs to be monitored, how to monitor that access, and whether a fee should be charged for accessing the beneficial ownership information, ensuring that any such fee is a reasonable amount so that it does not undermine the overall objective of establishing a public beneficial ownership register.

Important Considerations

- Enact provisions that clearly specify the beneficial ownership information that should be collected but protected from public access.
- Incorporate detailed provisions in laws and/or regulations regarding the grounds for applying for exemptions from public access to certain beneficial ownership information.
- Provide detailed guidance to companies and beneficial owners on the process for requesting this exemption.
- Incorporate provisions in the laws and/or regulations on the publication of statistical data relating to exemptions received, granted, rejected, and pending, and the reasoning for the decision.
- Ensure that no fee is charged for accessing the beneficial ownership data; however, if a fee is inevitable (e.g., to cover costs), it should be minimal, reasonable, and not restrictive.

E. Definition of Politically Exposed Persons and Their Reporting Obligations

Regarding politically exposed persons (PEPs), there are two legal and policy considerations for countries: (i) the definition of PEPs, and (ii) the beneficial ownership disclosure requirements for PEPs. These are discussed in detail below.

Definition of Politically Exposed Persons

PEPs, as defined under the FATF standards, are of three categories—domestic PEPs,[138] foreign PEPs,[139] and international PEPs,[140] including their family members and close associates. However, the terms "family members" and "close associates" are not defined by the FATF standards, and it has been left to countries to define these terms according to their own socioeconomic and cultural structure. To comply with international best practice, most countries provide working definitions or examples

---

[138]   The FATF Recommendations (as amended in March 2022) defines domestic PEPs as "individuals who are or have been entrusted domestically with prominent public functions, for example, Heads of State or of government, senior politicians, senior government, judicial or military officials, senior executives of state-owned corporations, important political party officials."

[139]   The FATF Recommendations (as amended in March 2022) defines foreign PEPs as "individuals who are or have been entrusted with prominent public functions by a foreign country, for example, Heads of State or of government, senior politicians, senior government, judicial or military officials, senior executives of state-owned corporations, important political party officials."

[140]   The FATF Recommendations (as amended in March 2022) defines international PEPs as "persons who are or have been entrusted with a prominent function by an international organisation" and refer to "members of senior management, i.e. directors, deputy directors and members of the board or equivalent functions."

of PEPs, as well as their family members and close associates who shall be treated as PEPs, in their laws and regulations, so that the scope of the terms is clear to the reporting entities and to other stakeholders.

Nonetheless, analyzing the legal and regulatory frameworks of the selected jurisdictions, this study finds that their definition of PEPs is not in compliance with international standards. For instance, in Mongolia, the PEP definition does not cover within its scope foreign PEPs and high officials of political parties, except election candidates.[141] In some jurisdictions, the definition of PEPs is not harmonized across different pieces of legislation and/or regulations. For instance, the definition of PEPs and its scope within the AML/CFT law might differ from the one provided in the law related to the extractive industries.

The lack of a clear and harmonized definition of PEPs in a country's legal and regulatory framework can result in leaving significant loopholes in the beneficial ownership disclosure regime, which can be exploited to hide the involvement of PEPs in legal persons as beneficial owners, and may thus undermine its effectiveness. This study therefore highly recommends that PEPs, their family members, and known close associates be clearly defined in the legislation, ensuring compliance with international standards. The definition of PEPs should also be harmonized across the various laws and/or regulations of a country, and "family members" and "known close associates" of PEPs should be included in that definition.

The EU Fifth AML Directive and the Natural Resource Governance Institute (NRGI) provide the basic language for defining PEPs, family members, and close associates (Box 6). This can be a useful guide for countries in the Asia and Pacific region when developing their PEP definition, ensuring compliance with international standards.

---

[141]   Dashdorj, E. 2022. *Considerations on Identifying and Reporting PEPs in Mongolia*. Presentation made during ADB and EITI Regional Workshop on Advancing Beneficial Ownership Transparency. 21– 23 February.

Box 6: The EU Fifth AML Directive and the NRGI Definition of Politically Exposed Persons

Article 3 of the Fifth AML Directive provides the following definition of PEPs, their family members, and known close associates:

(i)   "PEP" means a natural person who is or who has been entrusted with prominent public functions and includes the following: (a) heads of State, heads of government, ministers and deputy or assistant ministers; (b) members of parliament or of similar legislative bodies; (c) members of the governing bodies of political parties; (d) members of supreme courts, of constitutional courts or of other high-level judicial bodies, the decisions of which are not subject to further appeal, except in exceptional circumstances; (e) members of courts of auditors or of the boards of central banks; (f) ambassadors, chargés d'affaires and high-ranking officers in the armed forces; (g) members of the administrative, management or supervisory bodies of State-owned enterprises; (h) directors, deputy directors and members of the board or equivalent function of an international organisation. No public function referred to in points from (a) to (h) shall be understood as covering middle-ranking or more junior officials.

(ii)   "Family members" includes the following: (a) the spouse, or a person considered to be equivalent to a spouse, of a PEP; (b) the children and their spouses, or persons considered to be equivalent to a spouse, of a PEP; (c) the parents of a PEP.

(iii) "Persons known to be close associates" of PEPs means: (a) natural persons who are known to have joint beneficial ownership of legal entities or legal arrangements, or any other close business relations, with a PEP; (b) natural persons who have sole beneficial ownership of a legal entity or legal arrangement which is known to have been set up for the de facto benefit of a PEP.[a]

The NRGI states that the basic language for defining "PEP" should include the following:

(a)   an individual who is, or has been, entrusted with a foreign or domestic public function and includes — (i) a head of state or government, (ii) a minister; (iii) a deputy minister, (iv) an agent involved in sector administration, (v) a politician, (vi) a political party official, (vii) a judicial official or other senior official of a quasi-judicial body, (viii) a military official, or (ix) an SOE official;

(b)   an immediate family member of a person referred to in paragraph (a), including but not limited to a spouse, child, or parent; or

(c)   a close associate of a person referred to in paragraph (a).[b]

AML = anti-money laundering, EU = European Union, NRGI = Natural Resource Governance Institute, PEP = politically exposed person, SOE = state-owned enterprise.

Sources:

[a] EU 5th AML Directive, Article 3.
[b] Westenberg, E., and A. Sayne. 2017. Beneficial Ownership Screening: Practical Measures to Reduce Corruption Risks in Extractives Licensing NRGI Briefing. October. p. 12.

Beneficial Ownership Disclosure Requirements for Politically Exposed Persons

The FATF standards require that reporting entities subject to AML/CFT obligations under their domestic legislation be required to identify and verify the identity of PEPs, who can be either their customers or their beneficial owners, and to apply enhanced due diligence measures to PEPs. However, no specific obligation is placed on PEPs to disclose their status as a beneficial owner in a central beneficial ownership register established by countries, since the establishment of a beneficial ownership register is not a mandatory requirement under the FATF standards. Such a requirement also does not exist under the EU Fifth AML Directive, which requires the establishment of central beneficial ownership registers by the EU member states.

Nonetheless, a more stringent system of disclosure requirements is applied to PEPs by the EITI standard, since PEPs are deemed to be at higher risk because of their potential involvement in bribery and corruption by virtue of their position and the potential conflict of interest that might ensue in government contracting and licensing. The EITI standard specifically requires that if a PEP is a beneficial owner of a legal entity in the extractives sector, his or her status as a PEP must be declared and published in the beneficial ownership register or through other reporting mechanisms. The EITI requires countries to adopt reporting obligations for PEPs based on the types of prevalent corruption risks in the country.

In line with the EITI standard, it is widely recognized that the beneficial ownership disclosure requirements for PEPs should be kept extremely low, or at 0% ownership of shares or voting rights, which means that an individual who is a PEP should still be considered a beneficial owner of a legal entity regardless of his or her ownership or controlling interest. This is justified considering the influence and power PEPs derive from their positions, which can be abused for the purpose of corruption, bribery, and money laundering. Box 7 provides examples of the thresholds that various countries have established for PEPs to disclose their beneficial ownership information.

Box 7: Threshold for Politically Exposed Persons for Beneficial Ownership Disclosures—Country Examples

In Armenia, the threshold for PEPs was set at 0% for 2020 extractive industries' disclosures, which implies that the PEP status of beneficial owner(s) must be disclosed irrespective of the threshold.

A similar approach has also been taken by the Kyrgyz Republic, which requires that if the beneficial owner(s) of a legal person is a PEP, his or her status must be disclosed regardless of the size of their ownership stake in the legal entity.

Private, unlisted companies reporting material payments to the Government of the United Kingdom in accordance with the United Kingdom EITI are required to disclose information in relation to any PEPs, as part of their EITI reporting, where such PEPs directly or indirectly ultimately own or control more than 5% of a company or group.

In Ghana, PEP disclosures are differentiated between foreign PEPs and domestic PEPs. For foreign PEPs, the threshold for beneficial ownership disclosure is 5% and for domestic PEPs 0%. Although this study assumes that this differentiation between foreign and domestic PEPs regarding beneficial ownership disclosure might be based on the risk-based approach applied by Ghana, it nonetheless strongly recommends adopting a uniform beneficial ownership disclosure approach for both foreign and domestic PEPs, to avoid any loopholes.

EITI = Extractive Industries Transparency Initiative, PEP = politically exposed person.

Source: Author.

Important Considerations

- Adopt a single and uniform definition of politically exposed persons (PEPs) that complies with relevant international standards, and, if possible, include the necessary details on the different types of PEPs, their family members, and close associates, to provide more clarity and guidance to all stakeholders.
- Impose beneficial ownership disclosure requirements on PEPs, as a good practice, for all legal entities and all legal arrangements.

F. Sanctions and Penalties

A jurisdiction must have effective enforcement provisions and procedures in place, including adequate monitoring, and mandatory powers to ensure the effective implementation of the beneficial ownership disclosure regime. The Interpretative Note to Recommendation 24 clearly requires "effective, proportionate and dissuasive sanctions" to be imposed on legal or natural persons if they fail to properly comply with their beneficial ownership obligations.[142]

There is a lack of a clear approach and understanding among the selected jurisdictions as to what amounts to "effective, proportionate, and dissuasive" sanctions in the case of failure to comply with the beneficial ownership disclosure requirements. Mechanisms should therefore be put in place to ensure an effective enforcement of the beneficial ownership sanctions regime. Some jurisdictions, such as Kazakhstan, Indonesia, and Mongolia, do not have any specific penalties for violations related to beneficial ownership requirements; instead, there are general punishment provisions that may apply in these situations. On the other hand, a few jurisdictions provide for specific penalties for violations related to beneficial ownership requirements. They penalize typical violations, such as failing to provide the required information; submitting false, fraudulent, or misleading information; providing inaccurate, incomplete, or inconsistent information; general default or failing to comply with the requirements; failing to respond to information requests; or failing to update information. Even at the international level, several studies highlight that putting in place "effective, proportionate, and dissuasive" sanctions is one of the most common challenges faced by countries when implementing beneficial ownership transparency (BOT).[143]

In this section, this study highlights three major legal and policy considerations for jurisdictions when developing their beneficial ownership sanctions regime: (i) the types of conduct to be sanctioned, (ii) the types of sanctions, and (iii) the target or subject of sanctions. Another crucial issue, as discussed earlier, was the need to clearly determine the authority responsible for enforcing sanctions, as well as the need to ensure that the designated authority has sufficient resources, the legal mandate, and powers to enforce sanctions. With regard to developing a beneficial ownership sanctions regime and its enforcement, the Open Ownership principles can serve as useful guidance for countries (Box 8).

---

[142] See FATF Recommendations 2012. INR 24. para. 18.

[143] Footnote 13, p. 15.

Box 8: The Open Ownership Principles—Sanctions and Enforcement

- Effective, proportionate, dissuasive, and enforceable sanctions should exist for non-compliance with disclosure requirements, including for non-submission, late submission, incomplete submission, or false submission.
  Sanctions that cover the person making the declaration, the beneficial owner, registered officers of the company, and the declaring company should be considered.

- Sanctions should include both monetary and non-monetary penalties.

- Relevant agencies should be empowered and resourced to enforce the sanctions that exist for non-compliance.

- Data on non-compliance should be made available.

Source: Open Ownership. 2020. The Open Ownership Principles. Verification of Beneficial Ownership Data. Policy Briefing (May). p. 7. https://openownershiporgprod-1b54.kxcdn.com/media/documents/oo-briefing-verification-briefing-2020-05.pdf.

In line with Open Ownership Principles, this study recommends that all types of conduct be sanctioned, such as non-submission, late submission, incomplete submission, or false submission of the beneficial ownership information, and be covered within the beneficial ownership sanctions regime, and that this should also extend to include persistent non-compliance.[144]

The types of sanctions that should be enforced for breaches of beneficial ownership disclosure usually vary across jurisdictions, and include administrative, civil, and criminal sanctions.[145] Administrative sanctions include denial, revocation, or termination of a license or concession (Indonesia, Kazakhstan, the Kyrgyz Republic, and the Philippines), and the refusal to renew a license. Civil sanctions generally include fines, ranging from a low end of about $12.00 to $140 (Malaysia) and nearly $150 (Kazakhstan), to a mid-range of $2,000 to $4,000 (Albania), or $3,000 to $20,000 (Montenegro), up to a high-end of $63,000 (Belgium) (footnote 145). There are also a few countries, such as France and the UK, which differentiate the penalties applicable to individuals and companies. Criminal sanctions include criminal fines or imprisonment—for example, in the UK, this is up to 2 years.

---

144   See Open Ownership. 2021. Principles for Effective Beneficial Ownership Disclosure. https://www.openownership.org/en/principles/. July.

145   For more details on sanctions and enforcement for beneficial ownership disclosure regime, see Chhina, R., and T. Kiepe. 2022. Designing Sanctions and their Enforcement for Beneficial Ownership Disclosures. Policy Briefing. https://openownershiporgprod-1b54.kxcdn.com/media/documents/Designing_sanctions_and_their_enforcement_for_beneficial_ownership_disclosure.pdf.

A few jurisdictions also impose other types of nonfinancial sanctions that include preventing financial institutions and designated nonfinancial businesses and professions (DNFBPs) from forming business relationships or executing transactions with an entity that has failed to register or update its information in the central beneficial ownership register (North Macedonia) or making natural and legal persons who have failed to comply with the beneficial ownership disclosure requirements ineligible for government contracts (Box 9) (footnote 145).

Box 9: Sanctions—The Case of Slovakia

In Slovakia, if the beneficial ownership information registered in the Register of Public Sector Partners is found to be incorrect or incomplete, the designated authority can fine the company, remove them from the register, or cancel any current government contracts to which they are a party. Fines can be up to 100% of the economic benefit of a company's government contracts, or if that cannot be determined, up to €1 million. Authorized persons and those in management positions can be fined up to €100,000. Removal from the register means a company cannot undertake contracts with the government.

Source: Open Ownership. 2020. *Early Impacts of Public Registers of Beneficial Ownership: Slovakia.* Impact Story. September.

For sanctions to be effective, countries should ensure that a combination of different types of sanctions—financial, nonfinancial, and criminal sanctions—are available and applied by relevant authorities. Financial sanctions alone, even if they are in the high-end range, may be considered as an acceptable added cost by criminals who are engaging in illegal activities.[146] Therefore, as an overarching principle, countries' beneficial ownership sanctions regime should also include a combination of different types of sanctions, to enhance their effectiveness.[147]

Finally, another important consideration for countries in relation to sanctions and penalties is on whom to impose them. Liability is typically placed on the declarant in many jurisdictions, who may be either an individual or a company, depending on the law. Some laws, however, extend liability to company officers, which usually includes directors, the executive, and management of the company (e.g., in Denmark, Spain, Ukraine, Belgium, the UK, and France), or to the beneficial owner(s) of the company (e.g., in Austria, Luxembourg, Poland, and the UK) (Box 10).

---

[146]   Footnote 28, p. 14.
[147]   Footnote 115, p. 34.

Box 10: Example of Beneficial Ownership Sanctions Regime in the United Kingdom

In the United Kingdom, the following sanctions provisions targeting natural and legal persons are enacted under the Companies Act 2006 for breaches of beneficial ownership disclosure requirements:

If a beneficial owner fails to provide the required beneficial ownership information to the legal person within 1 month of receiving such a notice from the legal person, a beneficial owner may have his or her relevant shares restricted, meaning that all voting, dividend, and other share rights are suspended, and no transfers are permitted without a court order. Failure to provide information is also a criminal offense which is punishable with 2 years of imprisonment or a fine or both.

If anyone provides false information on beneficial owner(s), it is considered a criminal offense that is punishable with up to 2 years of imprisonment or a fine or both. Where a company commits the offense, the directors are also subject to criminal liability.

If the designated natural person of the company fails to take reasonable steps to identify beneficial owners or send notices to beneficial owners with regard to changes, such an individual is committing a criminal offense and is subject to up to 2 years of imprisonment or a fine or both.

If the company fails to maintain a beneficial ownership register or refuses a request to inspect the register, the company and its directors commit a criminal offense that is punishable by a fine.

Failure to submit changes in beneficial ownership information within a prescribed timescale is a criminal offense, which is punishable by a fine.

Source: Companies Act 2006, United Kingdom.

As a general principle, it is important to ensure that sanctions are available against both the natural persons (the beneficial owner, the person making the declaration, and officers of the company) and the legal persons (the company making the declaration) to ensure that the deterrent effect of sanctions applies to all the key persons and entities involved in the beneficial ownership disclosure.

Important Considerations

- Incorporate effective, proportionate, and dissuasive sanctions for different types of conduct that amount to a breach of beneficial ownership disclosure requirements.
- Enact a combination of financial, nonfinancial, and criminal sanctions in the beneficial ownership regime to increase their deterrent effect.
- Sanctions should be applied against both legal persons and natural persons, including the beneficial owner, the person making the declaration, and officers of the company, to ensure their effectiveness.

VI. Conclusions

The significance of BOT as a tool to fight corruption, money laundering, terrorist financing, tax evasion, and other forms of financial crime cannot be overestimated. For this reason, this topic is high on the agenda of many international institutions, including the FATF, the Global Forum, the EITI, and the UNCAC. All these international standard-setting bodies require countries to take adequate measures to promote and ensure the transparency of beneficial ownership within their jurisdictions. This study finds that countries face various challenges in ensuring efficient and effective national beneficial ownership regime and system, particularly in identifying and verifying the beneficial ownership information of corporate vehicles and preventing their misuse for criminal purposes.

This study has highlighted the ongoing reforms, challenges, and opportunities in selected Asia and Pacific countries for ensuring BOT, as well as best practices and practical guidelines for implementing beneficial ownership reforms. One of the crucial elements in driving the necessary beneficial ownership reforms within a jurisdiction is high-level political commitment and support for BOT, without which, it might not be possible to achieve the desired outcomes. This high-level political support can ensure adequate budgeting and resourcing (both human and technical) to push the agenda for BOT and to promote action. As is evident from this study, there are varying degrees of awareness and support for beneficial ownership reforms in the Asia and Pacific region, thus the BOT landscape has developed unevenly across countries in the region. PNG, for instance, has not yet imposed any legal obligation on legal entities to obtain and disclose their beneficial ownership information.

A few jurisdictions, such as Tajikistan and Timor-Leste, have taken initial steps in this regard, yet the laws and regulations are unclear and not fully developed for effective beneficial ownership disclosure. Kazakhstan and the Kyrgyz Republic have started collecting beneficial ownership information, but the information appears to be incomplete, inaccurate, and not available to the public. Indonesia has taken a significant step by establishing a centralized beneficial ownership registry, but is currently facing a challenge in ensuring the accuracy and currency of the beneficial ownership data, and in deciding whether the beneficial ownership information should be freely accessible to the public. Armenia has taken significant steps toward ensuring BOT by establishing an online beneficial ownership register, which has recently been expanded to include all sectors beyond the extractive industries. Armenia is currently working to strengthen the verification procedures and data quality in the online register, and improve the use and analysis of beneficial ownership information by relevant authorities and stakeholders.

Delivering access to reliable and up-to-date information on beneficial owners is important; however, the challenges involved in achieving that objective are substantial. The selected countries in this study have experienced some common challenges which they should analyze and address within their national legal and regulatory framework and systems to ensure BOT. These challenges include the need to (i) establish a sound and efficient beneficial ownership disclosure regime encompassing a clear, robust, and unified definition of "beneficial owner" set out in law; (ii) address the issue of bearer shares, nominee shareholders, and nominee directors; (iii) set up mechanisms to collect and verify beneficial ownership information; (iv) ensure public disclosure of the beneficial ownership data; (v) identify PEPs as beneficial owners and their reporting requirements; and (iv) establish effective sanctions and enforcement mechanisms. Related to these beneficial ownership issues, this study has highlighted best practices from various countries through examples and case studies.

To ensure BOT and to prevent the misuse of legal persons for criminal purposes, one of the key recommendations made by this study, in line with the FATF Recommendations 2012, is for countries to adopt a multipronged approach—that is, using multiple sources of information on beneficial ownership (a company approach, a registry approach, and an existing information approach) that should complement each other to ensure the adequacy and accuracy of the beneficial ownership information.

Establishing a register on beneficial owners of corporate vehicles, as one of the mechanisms for ensuring BOT, has been identified by this study as an emerging trend among jurisdictions. This has also been widely recognized as a best practice for ensuring that beneficial ownership information is available and accessible to competent authorities in a timely manner. A recent study by Transparency International, published in 2021, clearly highlights the usefulness and impact of beneficial ownership data in central beneficial ownership registers for investigators, the media, and civil society. Such information has been useful in uncovering conflicts of interest, exposing high-level corruption, tracking unexplained wealth, uncovering money laundering, and enhancing law enforcement efforts.[148] However, ensuring the adequacy and accuracy of the beneficial ownership data in this register requires that countries put in place various other mechanisms, including raising awareness among legal entities of the concept of beneficial ownership and their beneficial ownership disclosure requirements, and the significant role played by financial institutions, DNFBPs, and civil society.

Table 8 summarizes some of the key points for consideration by countries on various topics analyzed and discussed in this study in order to enhance BOT.

---

[148]   Transparency International. 2021. *Out in the Open: How Public Beneficial Ownership Registers Advance Anti-Corruption.* https://www.transparency.org/en/news/how-public-beneficial-ownership-registers-advance-anti-corruption; See also Transparency International. 2021. Response to FATF's Public Consultation on Revisions to *Recommendation 24.* August. pp. 16–21. https://images.transparencycdn.org/images/A-New-Global-Standard-on-Beneficial-Ownership-Transparency-Response-to-FATF-Consultation-August-2021.pdf.

Table 8: Important Points for Consideration on Beneficial Ownership Transparency

Legal and Regulatory Framework for Beneficial Ownership Disclosures

- Clearly incorporate the beneficial ownership disclosure requirements in the relevant legislation—whether in a stand-alone law on the beneficial ownership register or in an already existing law, depending upon the country's legal system and BOT policy goals. Ensure that all relevant legislation and/or regulations are amended accordingly to ensure certainty and uniformity in the approach. Establish an interagency working group to conduct a legal gap analysis on BOT requirements, and to propose and implement the necessary beneficial ownership reforms.

- Ensure that the definition of beneficial owner(s) includes within its scope both direct and indirect ownership and controlling interests, including natural persons who ultimately own or control or exercise ultimate effective control over legal entities or arrangements.

- Adopt a single, unified, and robust definition of beneficial ownership in the primary legislation—with potential variations in thresholds for disclosure by the extractives and non-extractives sectors—to minimize loopholes and to make it easier to produce corresponding forms for data collection.

- Ensure that a wide range of legal entities, including foreign entities, subsidiaries, and joint ventures, are included within the scope of the beneficial ownership disclosure requirements for the register. Any exemptions for beneficial ownership disclosure requirements for certain legal entities should be justified, considering the level of risk.

- Clearly identify the authorized persons responsible for disclosing the beneficial ownership information in the register.

- Clearly identify the authorities responsible for collecting, maintaining, and verifying the beneficial ownership information. This may include the company's registrar, the tax authority, or another designated authority, depending on the country's legal and institutional framework and national objectives for BOT.

- If the beneficial ownership data are to be collected and maintained by more than one authority or gency, the legal and regulatory framework should clearly designate the roles, responsibilities, and powers of each authority and should ensure effective cooperation between them, as well as the interoperability of the beneficial ownership data.

- Give adequate powers to authorities responsible for collecting, maintaining, and verifying the beneficial ownership data to ensure effective compliance with beneficial ownership disclosure requirements.

- Enact proper provisions in relevant laws and/or regulations to prohibit the issuance of new bearer shares or bearer share warrants, and to prevent the misuse of existing bearer shares or bearer share warrants.

- Take adequate measures to mitigate the risks associated with nominee shareholders and nominee directors, including imposing an obligation on them to self-identify as a nominee to the relevant legal entity as well as to the company registrar so that the information can be properly recorded in relevant registers.

continued on next page

Table 8 (*continued*)

Beneficial Ownership Data Collection and Disclosure

- Require legal persons to keep an in-house beneficial ownership register containing certain minimum beneficial ownership data, and to make the register available to the public.
- Specify certain minimum beneficial ownership information requirements that should be obtained, maintained, and updated by the reporting entities, as well as by the legal persons, in the beneficial ownership register.
- Specify a clear time frame in laws and/or regulations for legal persons to report and update the beneficial ownership information in the central beneficial ownership register.
- Incorporate a provision in the laws that requires the relevant designated authority to maintain the beneficial ownership information for a minimum 5-year period after the dissolution of the company, which can be extended to an additional 5 years in certain circumstances (e.g., detection or investigation of a criminal offense), in conformation with the data protection and privacy laws.
- Ensure that corporate vehicles are aware of the concept of beneficial ownership, its significance, as well as their beneficial ownership-related requirements, by arranging sufficient awareness-raising and outreach activities.

Beneficial Ownership Data Verification

- Provide clear guidelines to legal entities and reporting entities on the beneficial ownership data that should be obtained and maintained to understand the entire ownership and control structure of a legal entity or arrangement.
- Establish, both at the policy and technical levels, effective verification and validation measures at all three stages of the verification process: pre-submission, submission, and after submission of the beneficial ownership data.
- Apply a combination of different verification mechanisms at various steps to ensure their effectiveness.

Beneficial Ownership Registers and Public Disclosure

- Enact provisions that clearly specify the beneficial ownership information that should be collected but protected from public access.
- Incorporate detailed provisions in the laws and/or regulations on the grounds of applying for exemptions from public access to certain beneficial ownership information.
- Provide detailed guidance to companies and beneficial owners on the process for requesting this exemption.
- Incorporate provisions in the laws and/or regulations on the publication of statistical data relating to exemptions received, granted, rejected, and pending, and the reasoning for the decision.
- Ensure that no fee is charged for accessing beneficial ownership data; however, if a fee is inevitable (e.g., to cover costs), it should be minimal, reasonable, and not restrictive.

continued on next page

Table 8 (*continued*)

Politically Exposed Persons and Their Beneficial Ownership Reporting Obligations

- Adopt a single and uniform definition of PEPs which conforms with relevant international standards and, if possible, include the necessary details on the different types of PEPs, their family members, and close associates, to provide more clarity and guidance to all stakeholders.
- Impose beneficial ownership disclosure requirements on PEPs, as a good practice, for all legal entities and legal arrangements.

Beneficial Ownership Sanctions and Enforcement

- Incorporate effective, proportionate, and dissuasive sanctions in the law and/or regulations for different types of conduct that amount to a breach of beneficial ownership disclosure requirements.
- Enact a combination of financial, nonfinancial, and criminal sanctions in the beneficial ownership regime to increase their deterrent effect.
- Sanctions should be applied against both legal persons and natural persons, including the beneficial owner, the person making the declaration, and officers of the company, to ensure their effectiveness.

BOT = beneficial ownership transparency, PEP = politically exposed person.
Source: Author

Appendixes

1. List of Stakeholders Consulted for This Study

- Altynai Sydykova, consultant, World Bank, Kyrgyz Republic
- Emanuel Bria, country officer for Asia, EITI International Secretariat
- Erdenechimeg Dashdorj, Natural Resource Governance manager, Open Society Forum, Mongolia
- Frida Rustiani, secretariat of National Strategy for Corruption Prevention, Indonesia
- Lukas Alkan, head of National Secretariat, EITI, PNG
- Mark Burnett, senior advisor for Eurasia, EITI International Secretariat
- Mariya Lobacheva, programme director, NGO Echo, Kazakhstan
- Olesia Tolochko, country officer for Eurasia, EITI International Secretariat
- Shar Tsolomon, national coordinator, EITI, Mongolia
- Ferdian Ari Kurniawan, secretariat of National Strategy for Corruption Prevention, Indonesia

2. List of Speakers on the 2022 Regional Workshop on Advancing Beneficial Ownership Transparency in Asia and the Pacific

The workshop is co-organized by the Governance Thematic Group of the Asian Development Bank (ADB) and the EITI International Secretariat. The objectives of this workshop are to (i) gather beneficial ownership practitioners, including ADB staff, government officials, civil society, and private companies from countries in Asia and the Pacific; (ii) showcase the best practices so far, and discuss challenges; and (iii) provide peer learning, and exchange experiences.

- Andrew Irvine, Legal and Company Engagement director, EITI Secretariat
- Elizabeth Fiona Alpe, senior transaction support specialist (Integrity), Private Sector Operations Department, ADB
- Erdenechimeg Dashdorj, Natural Resource Governance manager, Open Society Forum, Mongolia
- Francesco Checchi, Regional Anti-Corruption adviser, UNODC

- Frida Rustiani, secretariat of National Strategy of Corruption Prevention, Indonesia
- Fridolin Berek, expert staff, Corruption Prevention at the National Secretariat of Corruption Prevention
- Gay Ordenes, Asia director, EITI Secretariat
- Hakim Hamadi, head of the Technical Assistance and Outreach Unit, The Global Forum
- Hiranya Mukhopadhyay, chief of Governance Thematic Group, Sustainable Development and Climate Change Department, ADB
- John Versantvoort, head, Office of Anticorruption and Integrity, ADB
- Jose Luis Syquia, principal public management specialist, Sustainable Development and Climate Change Department, ADB
- Kristine Gabuzyan, head, Department of Anti-Corruption Policy Development and Monitoring, Ministry of Justice (Armenia)
- Lee Robins, Enforcement and Service manager, Companies House, United Kingdom
- Louise Russell-Prywata, director, Policy and Advocacy, Open Ownership
- Maira Martini, research and policy expert, Corrupt Money Flows, Transparency International
- Mark Robinson, executive director, EITI
- Matthieu Salomon, senior governance officer, Natural Resource Governance Institute
- Nicholas Vail, senior policy advisor, Corporate Transparency and Register Reform at Department for Business, Energy and Industrial Strategy, United Kingdom
- Stephen Abbott Pugh, data and technology manager, Open Ownership
- Vincent Lazatin, national director, Bantay Kita

References

Asia/Pacific Group on Money Laundering (APG). 2017. *Anti-Money Laundering and Counter-Terrorist Financing Measures: Mutual Evaluation Report of Mongolia.* Sydney. September.

APG. 2018. *Anti-Money Laundering and Counter-Terrorist Financing Measures: Mutual Evaluation Report of Indonesia.* Sydney. September.

APG. 2019. *2nd Follow-Up Report: Mutual Evaluation Report of Mongolia.* Sydney. October.

APG. 2019. *Anti-Money Laundering and Counter-Terrorist Financing Measures: Mutual Evaluation Report of Philippines.* Sydney. October.

APG. 2021. *2nd Follow-Up Report: Mutual Evaluation Report of Philippines.* Sydney. August.

Barron, M. et al. 2021. *Beneficial Ownership in Mongolia: A Way Forward.* LTRC. September.

BDO Consulting. 2020. *Final Report: BO Study – Papua New Guinea.* December.

Bruun, B. 2017. *Mandatory Registration of Beneficial Owners.* Lexology. 31 May.

Chhina, R., and T. Kiepe. 2022. *Designing Sanctions and their Enforcement for Beneficial Ownership Disclosures.* Open Ownership Policy Briefing. April.

Eurasia Group on Money Laundering (EAG). 2018. *Mutual Evaluation Report of Kyrgyz Republic.*

EAG. 2018. *Mutual Evaluation Report of the Republic of Tajikistan.*

EAG. 2019. *Kyrgyz Republic: Second Follow-Up Report.* November.

EAG. 2021. *Republic of Tajikistan: Second Follow-Up Report.* June.

Extractive Industries Transparency Initiative (EITI). 2019. *Beneficial Ownership in Asia.* Oslo. February.

EITI. 2019. *Legal Approaches to Beneficial Ownership Transparency in EITI Countries.* Oslo. June.

EITI. 2019. The EITI Standard 2019: *The Global Standard for the Good Governance of Oil, Gas and Mineral Resources*. Oslo. 15 October.

EITI. 2021. *Validation of Requirement 2.5 – Armenia: Final Assessment by the EITI International Secretariat*. Oslo. 23 March.

EITI-Timor-Leste. 2019. *2019 Reconciliation Report*. Oslo.

Financial Action Task Force (FATF) (2012–2022).. 2022. *International Standards on Combating Money Laundering and the Financing of Terrorism and Proliferation*. Paris. March.

FATF (2013–2021). 2021. *Methodology for Assessing Technical Compliance with the FATF Recommendations and the Effectiveness of AML/CFT Systems*. Paris. October.

FATF. 2014. *Transparency and Beneficial Ownership*. Paris. October.

FATF. 2019. *Best Practices on Beneficial Ownership for Legal Persons*. Paris. October.

FATF and Egmont Group. 2018. *Concealment of Beneficial Ownership*. Paris. July.

Gegenheimer, G. A. 2021. *Recommendation Report to the Philippines: To Improve the Framework and Process on Obtaining Accurate and Up-to-date Beneficial Ownership Information*. Manila: Asian Development Bank. April.

Global Witness. 2018. *The Companies We Keep: What the UK's Open Data Register Actually Tells Us about Company Ownership*. July.

Global Witness and Open Ownership. *2017. Learning the Lessons from the UK's Public Beneficial Ownership Register*. October.

Government of the United Kingdom, Department for Business, Energy and Industrial Strategy. 2017. *Guidance for People with Significant Control over Companies, SOCIETATES EUROPAEAE, Limited Liability Partnerships and Eligible Scottish Partnerships*. June.

Government of the United Kingdom, Department for Business, Energy and Industrial Strategy. 2019. *Post Implementation Review of the People of Significant Control Register*. October.

G20 Anti-Corruption Working Group. 2021. *Anti-Corruption Accountability Report 2021*. Rome.

Harari, H. et al. 2020. Ownership Registration of Different Types of Legal Structures from an International Comparative Perspective: State of Play of Beneficial Ownership – Update 2020. *Tax Justice Network*. 1 June.

Ime, F., and L. Russell-Prywata. 2022. Beneficial Ownership Transparency and the Fight against Grand Corruption in *Nigeria. Open Ownership Blog*. 15 February.

Knobel, A. 2019. Beneficial Ownership Verification: Ensuring the Truthfulness and Accuracy of Registered Ownership Information. *Tax Justice Network*. 22 January.

Knobel, A. 2020. *Transparency of Asset and Beneficial Ownership Information*. FACTI [Financial Accountability Transparency and Integrity] Panel Background Paper 4. 19 July.

Lord, J., and K. Armstrong. 2020. *Beneficial Ownership Transparency and Listed Companies*. Open Ownership. September.

Marano, M.E., J. Argibay, and A. Falco. 2020. *Beneficial Ownership Registration. A Transversal Demand*. Argentina: Financial Transparency Coalition. December.

Martini, M. 2019. *Who is Behind the Wheel? Fixing the Global Standards on Company Ownership*. Transparency International. September.

MONEYVAL. 2015. *Anti-Money Laundering and Counter-Terrorist Financing Measures: Fifth Round Mutual Evaluation Report of Armenia*. Strasbourg. December.

MONEYVAL. 2018. *Anti-Money Laundering and Counter-Terrorist Financing Measures: Fifth Round Mutual Evaluations: 1st Regular Follow-Up Report of Armenia*. Strasbourg. July.

Organisation for Economic Co-operation and Development (OECD). 2001. *Behind the Corporate Veil: Using Corporate Entities for Illicit Purposes*. Paris.

OECD. 2018. *Peer Review Report on the Exchange of Information on Request: Indonesia*. The Global Forum on Transparency and Exchange of Information for Tax Purposes, Second Round.

OECD. 2018. *Peer Review Report on the Exchange of Information on Request: Kazakhstan*. The Global Forum on Transparency and Exchange of Information for Tax Purposes, Second Round.

OECD. 2018. *Peer Review Report on the Exchange of Information on Request: Philippines*. The Global Forum on Transparency and Exchange of Information for Tax Purposes, Second Round.

OECD. 2020. *Peer Review Report on the Exchange of Information on Request: Papua New Guinea*. The Global Forum on Transparency and Exchange of Information for Tax Purposes, Second Round.

OECD and Inter-American Development Bank. 2019. *A Beneficial Ownership Implementation Toolkit* Paris. March.

Open Extractives. 2021. *Relational Database Design Considerations for Beneficial Ownership Information*. Technical Guidance. 16 December.

Open Ownership. 2020. *Beneficial Ownership in Law: Definitions*. Policy Briefing. October.

Open Ownership. 2020. *Beneficial Ownership Transparency in Armenia: Scoping Study*. August.

Open Ownership. 2020. Briefing: The Case for Beneficial Ownership as Open Data. Policy Briefing. July 2017.

Open Ownership. 2020. *Early Impacts of Public Registers of Beneficial Ownership: Slovakia*. Impact Story. September.

Open Ownership. 2020. *Verification of Beneficial Ownership Data*. Policy Briefing. May.

Open Ownership. 2021. Armenia and Latvia Become First Countries to Publish Data in Line with the Beneficial Ownership Data Standard. *Open Ownership Blog*. September.

Russell-Prywata, L., and J. Lord. 2019. *Implementing Beneficial Ownership Transparency in the Kyrgyz Republic Extractive Sector: Findings and Recommendations*. Open Ownership. February.

Transparency International. 2021. Out in the Open: How Public Beneficial Ownership Registers Advance Anti-Corruption.

Transparency International. 2021. *Response to FATF's Public Consultation on Revisions to Recommendation 24*. August.

United Nations Office on Drugs and Crime (UNODC). 2020. *Beneficial Ownership Regulations and Company Registries in Southeast Asia*. 29 September.

Westenberg, E., and A. Sayne. 2017. *Beneficial Ownership Screening: Practical Measures to Reduce Corruption Risks in Extractives Licensing. Briefing*, Natural Resource Governance Institute. October. p. 12.

Willebois, E. et. al. 2011. *The Puppet Masters: How the Corrupt Use Legal Structures to Hide Stolen Assets and What to Do About It*. Washington, DC: World Bank; Vienna: UNODC.